F. E. McWILLIAM

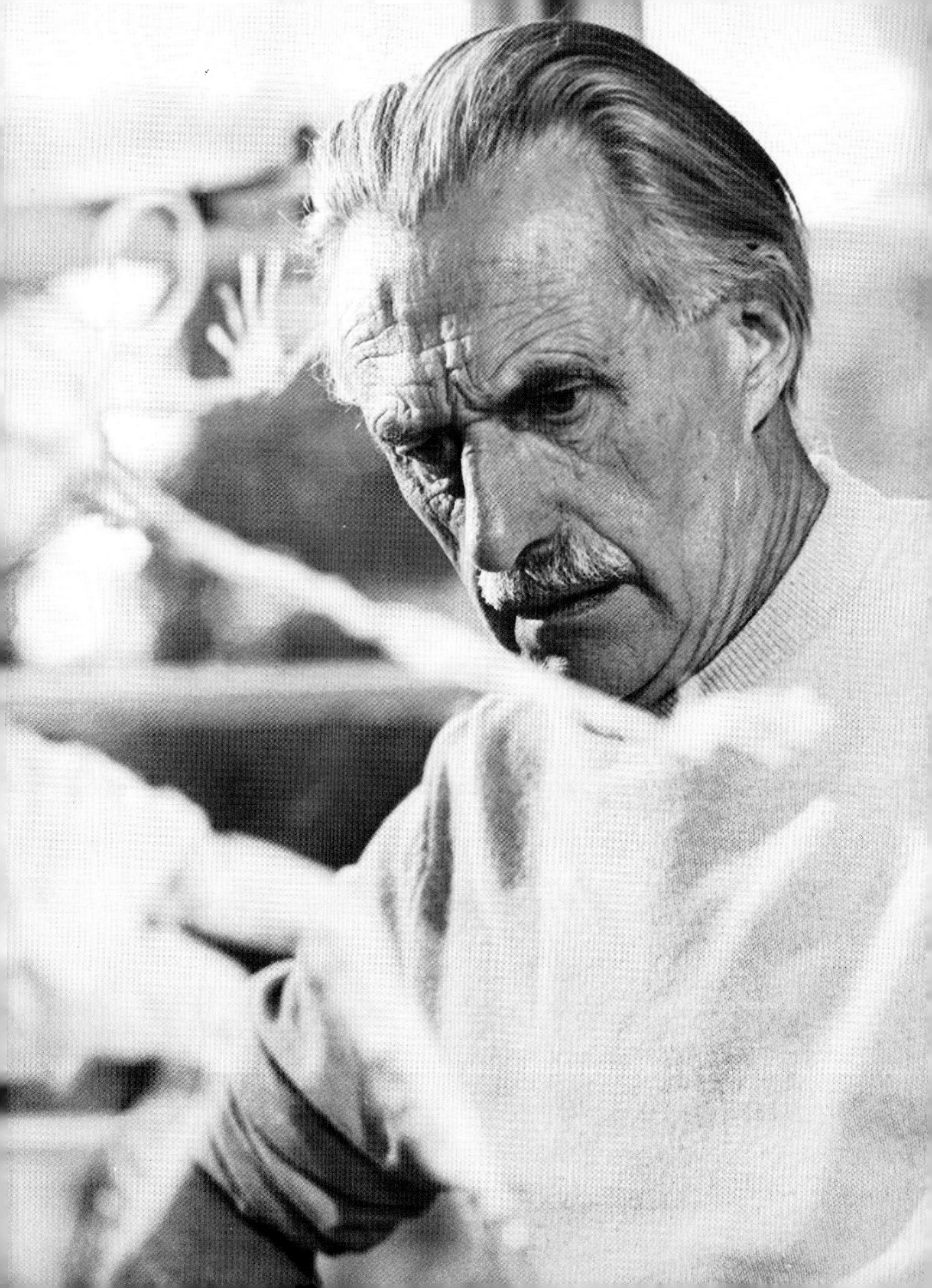

Mel Gooding

F. E. McWILLIAM
SCULPTURE 1932-1989

THE TATE GALLERY

cover
Two Forms 1938
cat.no.22

fronstispiece
F. E. McWilliam 1972

Photographic credits: James Austin,
F.E.McWilliam, Allied Irish Bank, David Brown
Fine Art Photographers (via Whitford & Hughes),
Eileen Tweedy (for Government Art Collections) and
Tate Gallery Photographic Dept.

ISBN 1 85437 016 2
Published by order of the Trustees 1989
for the exhibition of 10 May – 9 July 1989
Copyright © 1989 The Tate Gallery All rights reserved
Designed by Caroline Johnston
Published by Tate Gallery Publications,
Millbank, London SW1P 4RG
Typeset in Plantin and printed on Parilux matt 150gsm
by The Hillingdon Press, Uxbridge, Middlesex

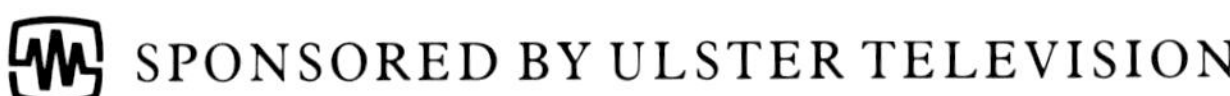

Contents

Foreword

We are delighted to be able to celebrate F. E. McWilliams's eightieth year with this, the first London retrospective exhibition of his work, covering a career which spans more than fifty years.

The selection has been made by Mel Gooding, art critic and writer, in very close collaboration with the artist. The exhibition concentrates on certain areas and themes in McWilliam's work and does not attempt to represent his whole and immensely varied output. Mel Gooding explains the rationale behind his selection in his introduction.

We very much appreciate Mel Gooding's work, both on the exhibition and on the catalogue. We are also grateful to all lenders who have so willingly agreed to support this show. Finally, I should like to thank Mr McWilliam himself. He has been unfailingly generous with both his time and his loans.

The exhibition has been sponsored by Ulster Television as part of their 30th anniversary year celebration. We are most grateful for their support.

Nicholas Serota *Director*

Introduction

I   A Portrait of the Artist

. . . I have never set any store by consistency – life is too short for restrictive practices – McWilliam

Although he studied painting at the Slade School, McWilliam had decided long before he left that his true vocation was that of sculptor. The encouragement of A. H. Gerrard, who taught sculpture at the School, was an important confirmation, but there was certainty about the young McWilliam's commitment that suggests a very deep predisposition. In conversation with Bryan Robertson, fifty years after carving the first work in the present exhibition, he recalled without hesitation modelling figures in plasticine as a favourite pastime of early childhood, and as providing his first experience of 'a sense of sculpture'. Pleasure in the heterogeneity of things, the infinite variety of the objects we encounter in life, and in the distinctive 'gear and tackle and trim' and differentiating disciplines of craftsmanship, have been central to McWilliam's life as an artist. His childhood in a small town in Northern Ireland was clearly formative in this respect:

> I think I was very lucky having been born where I was, in a country town. In those days everything was made in the town: Banbridge made most of the things it needed . . . Next door to our house was Carson the Cooper who made barrels, and of course we used to hide in them. They were actually made in the street, because Newry Street where I was born was a very wide street and people used to work in it. Then there was the shop that sold furniture where they made the furniture behind the shop . . . lovely smell of sawdust and everything. I loved going in and watching them. Opposite this was the rope maker man who made all the ropes for the harness people further up the street.

McWilliam's love of diverse materials may also be traced back to this early experience. He has carved in a great variety of woods, in limestone, cast stone and concrete; modelled in plastic wood and fibre glass as well as terracotta, clay, plaster and wax; he has worked with mosaic; and his bronze works have been cast from both modelled and assembled materials. Although a given material may by its nature spark off a set of new ideas, or suggest new possibilities of form and of subject, McWilliam has never been seriously inhibited by the doctrine of 'truth to materials'. This held that sculpture, and more particularly carving, should conform to the inherent qualities of the stone or wood out of which it was made, material which in Herbert Read's words 'has its own principles of form and structure'. Behind this lay a purist, and perhaps puritan, aesthetic that rejected disguise and simulation, and embraced naturalness and disclosure. McWilliam is sceptical: 'In the thirties this was the accepted slogan . . . but really it was a bit of a nonsense. . . . a useful phrase to explain why sculpture didn't have to be realistic.' His own work in fact has consistently played games with the materials of its making, going in for feats of balance and attenuation, for distortion and illusion.

Growing up in Ireland through an epoch of conflict confirmed in McWilliam a temperamental tendency to non-conformity and individuality. His approach to all things is marked by a spirited independence of judgement, tempered by an humane irony, and lightened by a highly developed sense of the absurd. His detestation of religious and political bigotry and the violence it breeds is absolute; it is matched by an aversion for highly organised and exclusive sects, cliques, coteries and institutions, social, political, artistic or otherwise. McWilliam has belonged to no movement, subscribed to no *ism*: like Stephen Dedalus (himself named after a sculptor-craftsman) McWilliam determined early to leave Ireland, with its political entanglements and demands for sectarian commitment, behind him. He would 'try to fly by those nets' and, to paraphrase Stephen's words, he 'would try to express himself in some mode of life or art as freely and wholly as he could. . . .' ('When I lived in Ireland', McWilliam has said 'I only wanted to get out of it to where the action in the visual arts was – Paris'.)

Inevitably, this inherent disposition, so shaped by the place and circumstances of his upbringing, has deeply affected McWilliam's practice as an artist. He has taken what he wanted from many sources, turning to his own ends the discoveries and inventions of his greatest contemporaries, Brancusi, Arp, Giacometti, Picasso. He was liberated as an artist by Abstraction, and exploited his new-found freedom to create a basically figurative surreal imagery that was uniquely his own, whilst, like his closest friends, Henry Moore and Ceri Richards, he reserved the right to move outside and beyond allegiance to the Surrealist Movement. Above all he has refused to maintain any fidelity to the notion of stylistic consistency, obeying without compunction an inner compulsion to try something different, explore new ground, to change direction and medium without regard to art world fashion or critical response.

This creative restlessness, and the stylistic variability that follows from it in McWilliam's work, have their disadvantages. Not every line of experiment has been equally creatively fruitful; taking risks and constantly embarking upon something new is an unpredictable business, and it is not surprising that there have been passages in his career when his work has lacked the absolute imaginative certainty of the carvings of the 'thirties, say, or the conceptual and formal resolution of the horizontal figures of the early 'sixties, or the fanciful originality of the 'Beans'. Few of the mosaic pieces were wholly successful, leaving aside the technical problems that the medium presented; and the 'Banners' of the mid-'seventies, lacking the sustained passion of the 'Women of Belfast' series which immediately preceded them, relied too heavily upon the interplay of verbal and visual elements, being in some cases little more than three-dimensional political cartoons. There are certain works of the 'fifties, also, in which McWilliam seems, uncharacteristically, to have tuned into a prevailing sculptural mood of melodramatic portent, with its typical formal emphasis upon the broken surface and figurative distortion. There is room here for critical debate, surely; but whatever individual preferences there may be for this or that period in his work, there can be no doubt of the extraordinary originality of McWilliam's vision or of the fecundity of his sculptural imagination. These fertile propensities prompted Penrose's observation: 'McWilliam is an inventor of styles.'

The habitual denial of identifiable style is a component of McWilliam's modernity. It places him in that line of modernism that is concerned with the elimination of expression, that sees art as a mode of inquiry, a means to the investigation of the world and the interrogation of reality. For all their profound differences, that definition of art as an heuristic procedure is something that surrealism shared with constructivism: both sought a revelation of a reality that lay behind the veil of appearances, and considered its disclosure to be necessary to human progress. For the constructivists that reality was to be found in the non-objective metaphysical and spiritual universals made accessible by geometric or otherwise rigorously principled procedures; for the surrealists it was identified as the marvellous immanent in the everyday, and discoverable through dreams and automatism. Both were supported by a great deal of philosophical, or pseudo-philosophical, rationalising and argumentation: the mid-'thirties was a period of noisy and often confused critical debate between their conflicting claims for allegiance, and those of the realists and socialist realists. Whilst maintaining an uncompromising political humanism, which has persisted to this day, McWilliam was not interested in the philosophical wrangles or the group participations that went with them.

As I have implied, however, as an artist he was operating at the heart of the modern movement; and it is to a modernist aesthetic that he has committed himself throughout his career. The artistic principles that have informed McWilliam's practice are complex and eclectic, and they have never been systematically articulated by the artist. He has resolutely steered clear of ideological and theoretical formulations; he has written next to nothing. Like Stephen Dedalus he has resorted to 'silence, exile, and cunning'. McWilliam's creative intelligence, speculative and ironic, has ranged freely over artistic, philosophical, scientific, moral and political issues: the outcomes of his contemplations are realised concretely, in his works, in poetic images, in the language of metaphor and correspondence.

II   The paradoxical activity

. . . we wish to create worlds as real as, but other than the world that is. – John Fowles

There is nothing in his output which suggests that McWilliam was ever interested, as a sculptor, in constructive art (though the house he helped to design for himself in 1936 had much of the so-called New Architecture about it, and part of the attraction of its site was the proximity of a splendid building by Maxwell Fry); the white painted sycamore carving ('Figure' cat. 16) which so impressed Nicholson in 1937 (exhibited in that year, significantly, as 'Two Circles') may have looked rigorously abstract in the company of the white reliefs and the sculptures and paintings of Nicholson, Hepworth and their circle, but placed (as it actually was in the AIA exhibition) in the context of surrealist imagery, its mysterious figurative presence, that of an idol-like *personnage*, is immediately manifest. Historically speaking, it is within that section that the piece truly belonged, for McWilliam has certainly owed more to surrealism, and is temperamentally more attuned to its modes of procedure, than to any other specific manifestation of the modernist spirit.

The mode of abstraction to which McWilliam was first attracted was that of the biomorphic reduction of figurative forms, of which approach Arp was the principal exponent, and that was being explored at the same time by Moore and Hepworth among others. The severe essentialising of Brancusi provided for this generation a liberating example. Biomorphic abstraction was very much in the air throughout the late 'twenties and 'thirties and to talk of influences within a general climate is of little critical value. We have a situation in which various artists, at quite different stages of their careers, were resorting to a common imagery that satisfied in different ways the particular requirements of their research. For sculptors, involved in that most difficult of arts, the simplification of forms that this kind of generalising and analogising reduction made possible was clearly felt as a release from a constricting and historically worn-out naturalism, itself based upon debased and sentimental classical conventions. It made possible a kind of rhythmic visual poetry, freed from precise description.

There can be no doubt that this insistent recurrence of organic abstract imagery in the modernist sculpture of this period (and also, incidentally, in the painting of the time) was an expression of a prevalent secular humanism, whose philosophical set was a principal determinant of the political and moral *ambience* of the art of the time. The biomorphic figure suggests the affinity of the human with other natural forms: 'For example', wrote Henry Moore in 1937, 'rounded forms convey an idea of fruitfulness, maturity, probably because the earth, women's breasts, and most fruit are rounded . . . I think the humanistic organic element will always be for me of fundamental importance in sculpture, giving sculpture its vitality'. More than this, the vague anatomies of the biomorphic propose that behind the particular and diverse actualities of the human body there is an archetypal human morphology, a quintessence of the physically human, not of a specifically realised ideal form as in Greek sculpture, but democratically potential and dynamic. As such it might also be seen as a metaphor for the unconscious, an indicator of the unity that underlies our disparate and fragmented conscious 'realities'. It has the indeterminate form of bodies in dreams. It was this aspect that accounted for its appeal to surrealist artists.

McWilliam, whilst he may have seen the force of these ideas and shared the values they implied, was uniquely ironic in his treatment of this pervasive formal language. He regarded it as but one of any number of possible means to an end, and felt free to extend the formal and thematic limits of the biomorphic, to complicate it, add to it, pun with it, make fun with it. The stone carvings of the late 'thirties adapt it to comic as well as grimly satiric purposes, whilst the 'Beans' of nearly thirty years later represent the furthest extreme of a playful refusal to treat elemental or archetypal forms with reverential solemnity. By then, of course, McWilliam had shown, in the series of horizontal figures of the early 'sixties, that he was equally capable of poetic and revealing improvisations with mechanomorphic forms.

It was especially important to the critical protagonists of modernist sculpture that biomorphic imagery made possible new departures in direct carving, which for various reasons, and with a powerful and fervent body of critical apologetics behind it, was enjoying an energetic revival as the quintessential sculptural art. 'Direct carving is the true road to sculpture', Brancusi had said. 'A figure carved in stone is fine carving when one feels that not the figure, but the stone through the medium of the figure, has come to life' wrote Adrian Stokes, whose refined and psychologically-charged distinction between carving and modelling was highly influential amongst the Hampstead modernists. Herbert Read could 'not avoid quoting' that passage from Stokes's *The Stones of Rimini* of 1934 in his *Appreciation* of Henry Moore which Zwemmer published in the same year. Although it would not be fair to say that Read accepted without qualification the near-mysticism of Stokes's exultation of carving ('Carving creates a face for the stone, as agriculture for the earth, as man for woman.'), his advocacy of what he himself called the 'almost ethical injunction' of 'truth to material' depended a great deal upon the historical dignity that Stokes bestowed upon the activity. What was being claimed for carving (and in this again we may discern the crucial influence of Brancusi) was nothing less than that by its alliance with natural materials and their timeless rhythms and forms, it disclosed the ideal and the universal. It enabled the artist to 'escape from what is incidental in nature,' in Read's words, 'and create what was spiritually necessary and eternal.'

As we have seen, McWilliam remained sturdily unimpressed by all this. He had no doubts of his friend Moore's genius, but he would 'admire and do otherwise.' Whereas for Moore (and this was as much a matter of temperamental predisposition as of philosophical disposition) the biomorphic led naturally to the monumental, towards the stasis of completeness and resolution, for McWilliam it led in a contrary direction altogether, towards kinetic indeterminacy. What appealed to McWilliam was its tendency to ambiguity, unpredictable analogy and oneiric equivocation. With a remarkable rapidity and directness, in his carvings of the 'thirties he identified the two central themes of his art: metamorphosis as a metaphor for the inescapable mutability of human experience; and visual correspondence and analogy as a sign of the hidden dynamics that animate all things, and whose material manifestations are a matter of marvellous chance among an infinitude of possibilities. It is precisely the 'incidental in nature' that has fascinated McWilliam; like Stokes's 'modeller' he 'imbues spatial objects with the animus and calculation of inner life'.

The incidental and the accidental have provided McWilliam with much of the impetus for his work; and his willingness to turn to his advantage what fate and chance may send his way, and the imaginative and technical capacity so to do, are abiding features of his creative procedure. Behind the unlikely and awkward inventions of his sculpture lies an attitude towards reality, a philosophy of Chance:

things could be thus; it is a matter of accident that they are not so. Art is a process of magical transformation by which whatever exists may be imagined and imaged as something else. It is a view of things that has much in common with that of Buñuel, another artist whose clear-sighted humanism was profoundly coloured by surrealism: 'Chance governs all things: necessity, which is far from having the same purity, comes only later . . . It isn't necessary that the world exists, that we be here living and dying. We're the children of accident; the universe could have gone on without us until the end of time'. In the interview with Bryan Robertson already quoted, McWilliam said, 'I don't want to get too philosophical about this but I happen to believe in an infinite universe, one with no beginning and no end; nothing else makes sense . . . Our life and death cycle, to which we are geared, is a continual evolvement. To me all art is a protest against this, against death, and an attempt to make something finite and lasting when actually *nothing is finite and lasting – only change. Art is a paradoxical activity'*.

In the post-war years Moore and Hepworth responded vigorously to increasing calls to provide a public art, in a language of sculpture that was new to the city square and skyscraper forecourt, and modernly 'abstract', but which consciously sought to restore to the art its traditional *gravitas* and grandeur of rhetorical function, in its privileged role as the signifier of social and moral certainties. McWilliam, on the other hand, persisted in art as play, in the exploitation of the fantastic and the fanciful, in the making of poetic fictions, inexplicable hypotheses. Reality was still to be ambushed by surprise, chanced upon by means of unpredictable juxtapositions, and the imagery that made this possible was most likely to be discovered in what might present itself to the artist when he was least expecting it. For McWilliam has been unashamedly open to what Stravinsky in his schoolmasterish way admonished as 'that capriciousness of imagination that is commonly called fancy. Fancy implies a predetermined will to abandon one's self to caprice'. In practical terms this has meant that the found object or the chance encounter has more often than not provided the idea, the image and the theme for exploration, improvisation and transformation. Such a procedure, validated by Surrealism, cannot help but be subversive of the dignity of sculpture as traditionally practiced. Picasso, in the fantastic transmogrifications of scrap materials of 1950 and 1951, and Miró, in his bronzes, are the greatest exponents of this essentially anarchic mode: McWilliam has admired both.

McWilliam, then, has been continuously aware that paradoxical, contradictory and alogical images are profoundly revelatory; like jokes, slips of the tongue, dreams, they are signals from the invisible and normally inaccessible hinterland of our waking reality. Moreover, to paraphrase an observation of Buñuel's, being inseparable from chance, they are invested with mystery. For McWilliam that is a quality in things that is of the deepest significance. 'Mystery' he has said, 'is terribly important, in art as in religion. I mean if you take mystery out of religion, you're only left with morality, and if you take the mystery out of art you're only left with design or illustration. *But what mystery is . . . is another matter'*. McWilliam has spent a lifetime paying homage to the inexplicable, accepting the reality of mystery, living with the paradox of art.

A Biographical Chronology

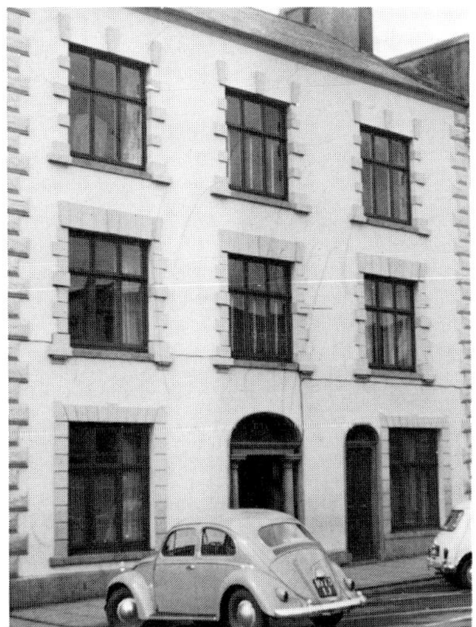

The artist's birthplace, Newry Street, Banbridge, Co. Down

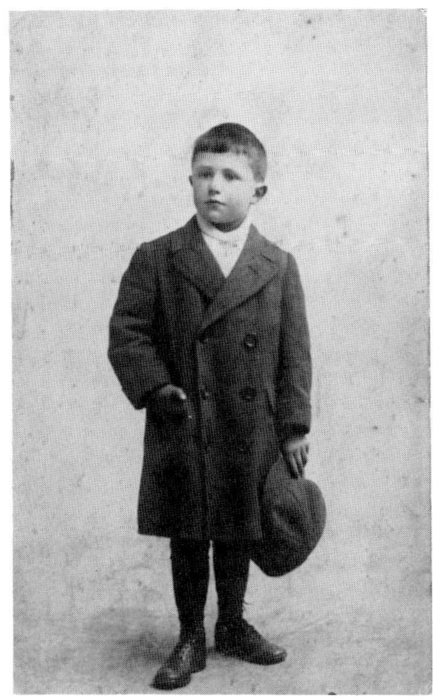

F. E. McWilliam, aged six, 1915

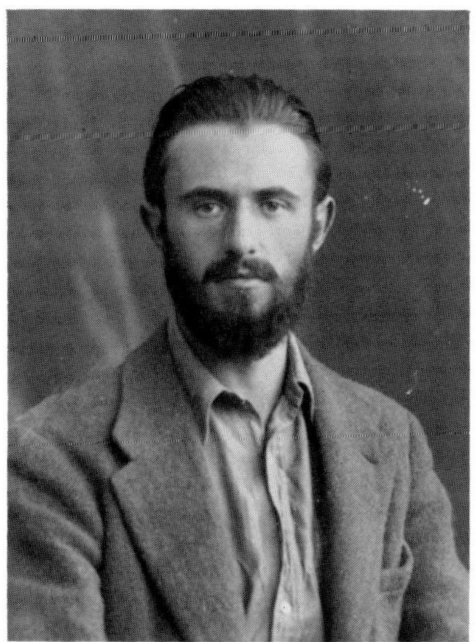

McWilliam, *Carte d'Identité* photograph, France, 1932

1909

Frederick Edward McWilliam was born in Newry Street, Banbridge, Co. Down, Ireland, on 30 April, the son of Dr William McWilliam, a general practitioner. Banbridge in the years before World War I was a small self-contained country town, mainly devoted to the manufacture of linen. Next door to the family home was the local cooper's workshop, and nearby in the street were the carpenters, who made furniture for the local people, and ropers and harness makers. 'It was a fascinating place for a small boy to grow up, and I think it had a bearing on my subsequent activities because of the constant sight of crafts-manship in action: not only seeing furniture being made, and harness, and rope, but the whole idea of people making things with their hands.'

There was a darker side to this experience, which has remained with the artist: 'I left Ireland when I was eighteen, and although I seldom return, what happens there concerns me closely; not just because most of my friends and relations are there, but because my early roots remain unbroken – especially the roots of memory. I can recall clearly what happened in my home town during the former "troubles". This left me with a lasting awareness and hatred of intolerance and religious bigotry'.

1928

After a period at Belfast College of Art, McWilliam left Ireland to study in London at the Slade School of Fine Art. Here he came under the formidable academic regime of Professor Tonks, with its emphasis upon systematic and rigorous drawing from the figure. During a tutorial on work which demonstrated an awareness of Cézanne, McWilliam was told by Tonks, 'Forget about that man; couldn't draw!' During this period, through the influence especially of A. H. Gerrard (later Slade Professor of Sculpture) his interest turned more particularly towards sculpture, but at the school this was still regarded as an optional secondary study. During his second year at the Slade he met, for the first time, Henry Moore, who was to be a lasting friend and influence.

A contemporary at the Slade was Beth Crowther, whom he was to marry in 1932.

1931

Awarded the Robert Ross leaving scholarship, McWilliam travelled to France, intending to live and study in Paris: 'It was the mecca, and the whole atmosphere testified to this; holy ground, full of the memories of Cézanne, and the presence of Picasso'.

He worked first as a labourer on a farm at Salernes, near Draguignan in Var, before moving to Paris, where he

took a studio at Port d'Orléans. In
Paris he met Zadkine and visited his
studio. Roger Hilton and Ithell Col-
quhoun were also in Paris at this time.
For practical reasons McWilliam con-
centrated at this time on painting,
although his commitment to sculpture
was by now determined. In Paris he
first encountered surrealism. More
importantly for him at the time, he
purchased at Sylvia Beach's *Shake-
speare and Company*, a copy of Joyce's
Ulysses, still banned in England.
Joyce and Shaw were abiding influences on McWilliam's outlook
upon things: Shaw for his direct
moral and political honesty, his complete lack of humbug; Joyce for his
complexity, his richness of reference;
both for their wit.

1932-1933

Great Britain came off the Gold Stan-
dard. The collapse of the pound
which followed forced McWilliam's
return to England. Newly married, he
moved to Chartridge in Buckingham-
shire. More or less isolated from
direct influences and artistic group-
ings, Beth continued to paint, and
Mac began in earnest to carve in
wood, especially cherrywood from the
orchards that surrounded the house
(see 'Mother and Child' cat.1;
'African Figure' cat.2; 'Figure' cat.3;
'Man and Wife' cat.4 etc.).

1936

In June he visited the *International
Surrealist Exhibition* at the New Bur-
lington Galleries, an event of great importance to the artist. McWilliam was
impressed above all by Magritte's
'The Red Model', the painting in
which a pair of boots is metamorphos-
ing into feet.

In September the McWilliams moved
to Steele's Road, Hampstead, close to
the Parkhill Road studios where
Moore, Read, Nicholson and Hepworth, among others, lived and
worked. Roland Penrose, who
became a friend during this period,
also lived nearby, as did Paul Nash.

1937

In the spring, at the suggestion of
A. H. Gerrard, McWilliam, Henry
Moore and Gerrard, accompanied by
their wives, made the journey to Hoptonwood Quarry in Derbyshire 'to
look for irregularly shaped pieces:
these were cheaper and more in-
teresting than the regular blocks more
usually supplied to professionals'.
Several important sculptures were to
be made from the stone gathered on
this occasion (see 'Two Forms'
cat.22; 'Mandible' cat.23; 'Eye, Nose
and Cheek' cat.25; 'Spanish Head'
cat.26 etc.).

In March/April he exhibited three
works ('Figure' 1937, exhibited as
'Two Circles', cat.16; 'Hollow
Figure' 1936, cat.14; and a painting,
'Composition' n.d.) at *The First
British Artists' Congress for Peace, For
Democracy, For Cultural Progress*
organised by the Artists International
Association in Grosvenor Square.
These were shown in the Surrealist

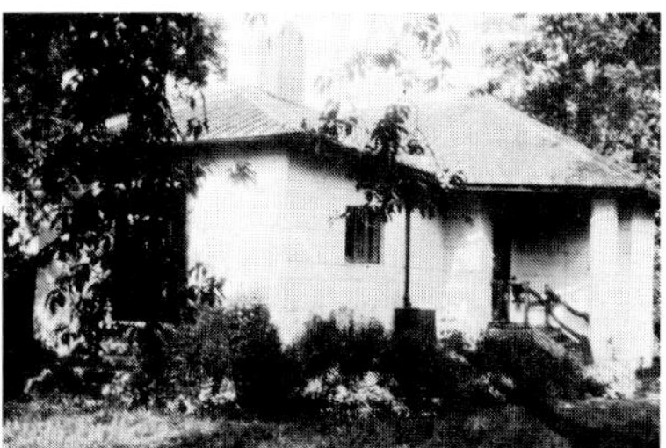

The house at Chartridge, 1934

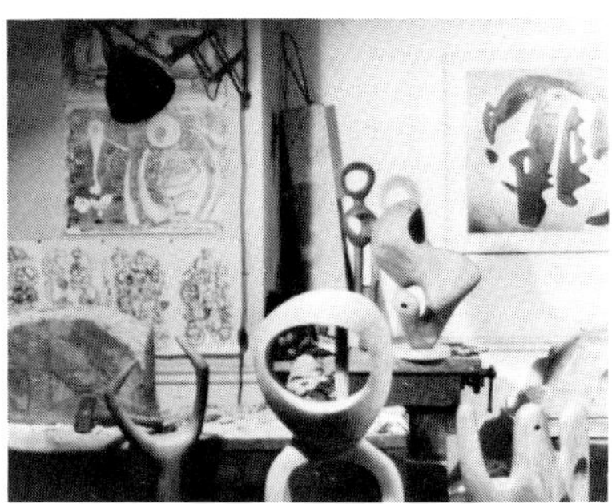

Studio, Steele's Road, Hampstead, 1936

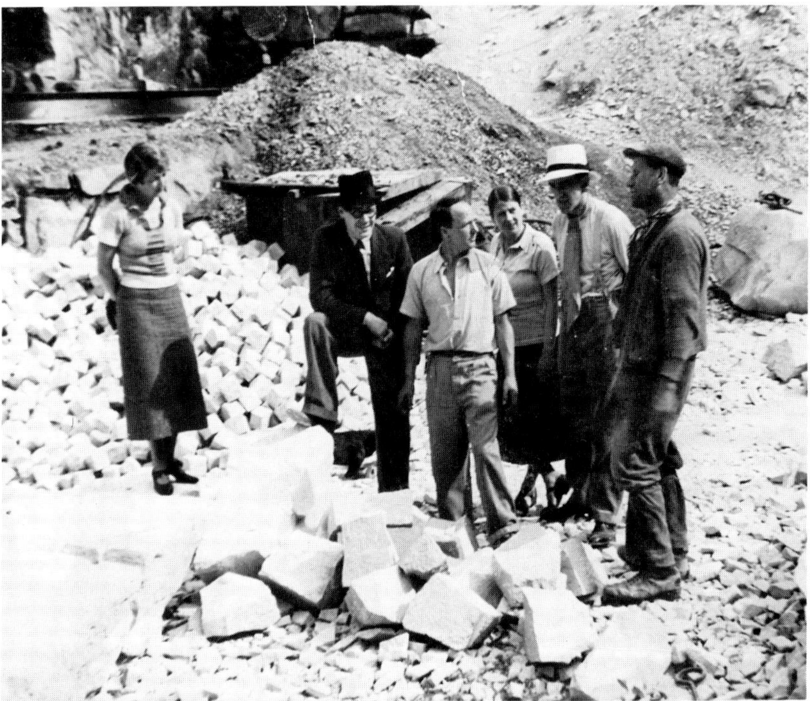

At Hoptonwood Quarry, Derbyshire, Spring, 1937.
Left to right: Irina Moore, Quarry Manager, Henry Moore,
Beth McWilliam, A. H. Gerrard, and a Quarryman
(photo by McWilliam)

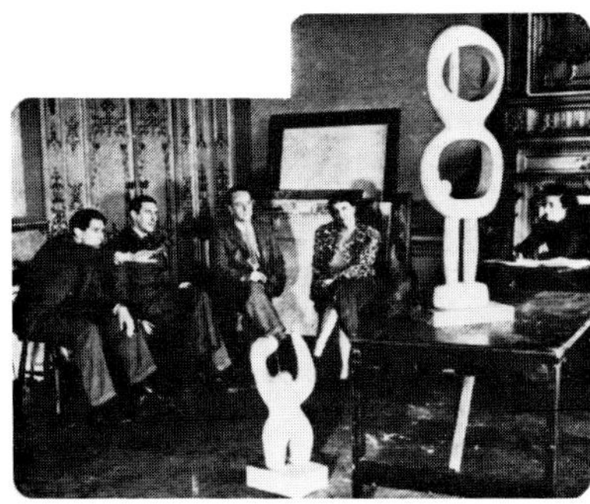

Selecting for the AIA British Artists' Congress Exhibition, Surrealist Section, 1937. Left to right. Roland Penrose, Paul Nash, Henry Moore, Naomi Durell. The sculpture is 'Figure' 1937 (cat. 14)

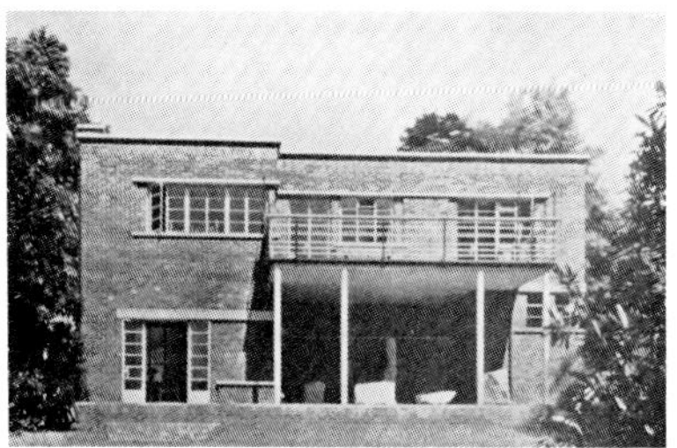

The house at New Malden shortly after completion (photo from *The Architect and Building News*, May 27 1938)

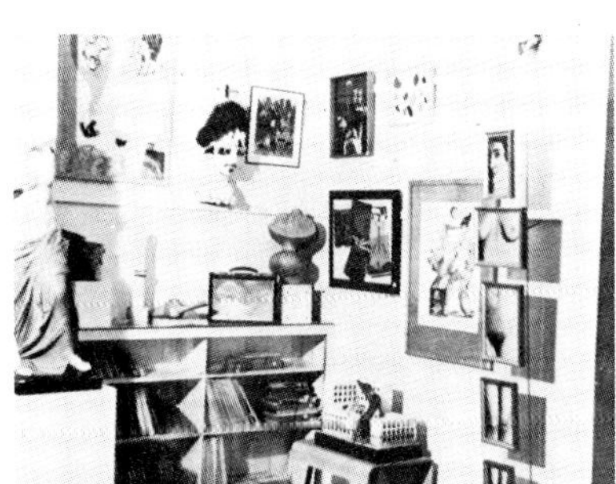

A view of *Surrealist Objects and Poems* exhibition at the London Gallery, December, 1937. McWilliam's 'object' is in the foreground. Magritte's 'L'Evidence Eternelle' can be seen to the right

Section, the exhibition being organised along lines of stylistic and group allegiances, and this effectively began McWilliam's association with the British Surrealist Group, which had been formed in 1936 at the time of the International Surrealist Exhibition in London. 'My work up to then had been mainly of an organic/abstract nature and I could have shown in the Abstract Section, but I chose the Surrealist camp because of its more liberal, non-doctrinaire attitude . . . But it would be true to say that I remained more a fellow traveller than a zealot.' Ben Nicholson had offered to reproduce 'Figure' 1937 (cat. 16) in *Circle: international survey of constructivist art* on condition that McWilliam showed it in with the Abstract Section. When Penrose was then offered 'Hollow Figure' for the Surrealist Section (characteristically, McWilliam was at first prepared to show with both abstractionists *and* surrealist

contingents), he promptly said 'We'll have them both!' McWilliam's work was not featured in *Circle*. Paul Nash became a friend at this time.

July: McWilliam moved to a house designed to his own requirements in collaboration with the architect H. A. Townsend, a friend since student days. Architecture was, and remains, a major interest. 'I'd have liked to have been an architect. I always thought that modern artists should live in modern houses.'

November: he contributed to the *Exhibition of Surrealism* at Gordon Fraser Gallery in Cambridge, and later in same month made a 'surrealist object' 'The big bird dies in town' for the exhibition of *Surrealist Objects and Poems* at E.L.T. Mesens's London Gallery in Cork Street.

Birth of daughter Sarah.

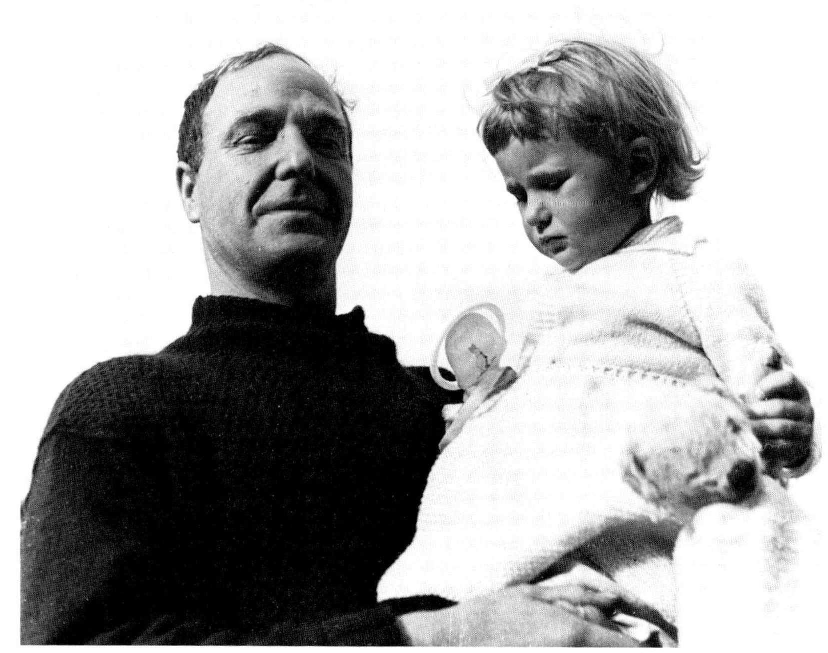

Henry Moore with Sarah McWilliam, 1938

1938

McWilliam made the Chamberlain masks worn by James Cant, Julian Trevelyan and Roland Penrose on the May Day demonstration in London. Began to attend meetings of the Surrealist Group. Friendship began with London-based surrealist-affiliated American artist Charles Howard, with whom he exchanged works.

Walking tour with Beth through the Black Forest.

1939

Exhibited in *Living Art in England* exhibition at London Gallery; invited to cite allegiance, he described himself in catalogue as 'Independent'.

First one-man show, at London Gallery, of sculpture and mono-print drawings. Introduced in *London Bulletin*, Mesens's magazine, which also included the catalogue of the exhibition, by Paul Nash: 'As a sculptor he comes of the breed of Brancusi rather than from the Maillol family. His ancestors are not far to seek but they neither inhibit nor inhabit his work. He has looked at the beauty of Giacometti, yet made his own tenuous beauty. He has submitted himself to the powerful influence of Henry Moore without, apparently, becoming hypnotized. He has left Laurens behind. And now, I think he is beginning to emerge'. (*London Bulletin* No.11 March 1939.)

Birth of daughter Bridget.

1940

June-July: exhibited 'Profile' (cat.19) in *Surrealism Today* at Zwemmer Gallery.

Joined Royal Air Force. Stationed at Kidbrook, Woolwich, and subsequently at Medmenham, mainly engaged on interpretation of aerial reconnaissance photography.

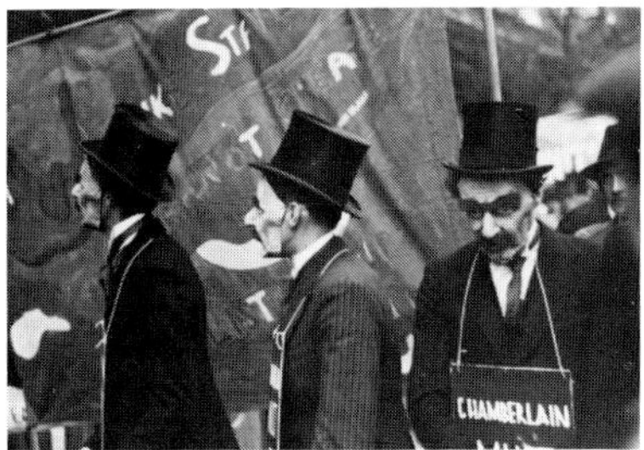

May Day demonstration, 1938. Chamberlain masks by McWilliam. Left to right: Julian Trevelyan, Roland Penrose, James Cant

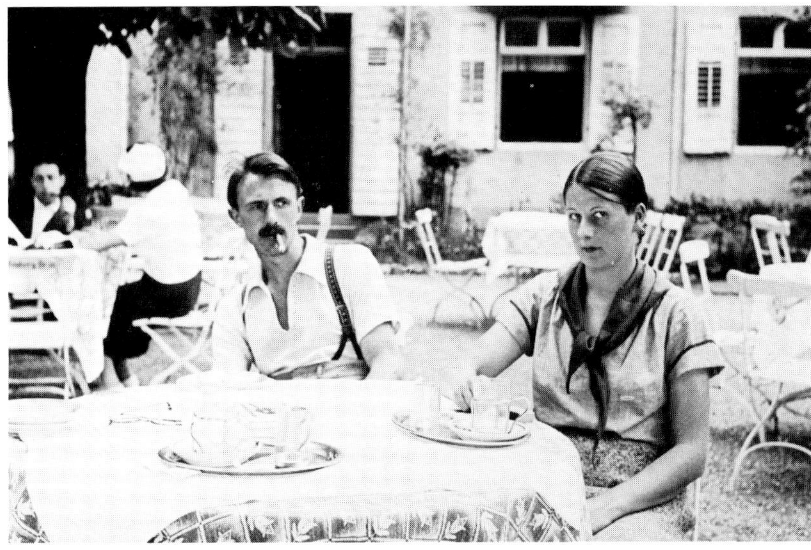

Mac and Beth McWilliam, Freiberg, 1938

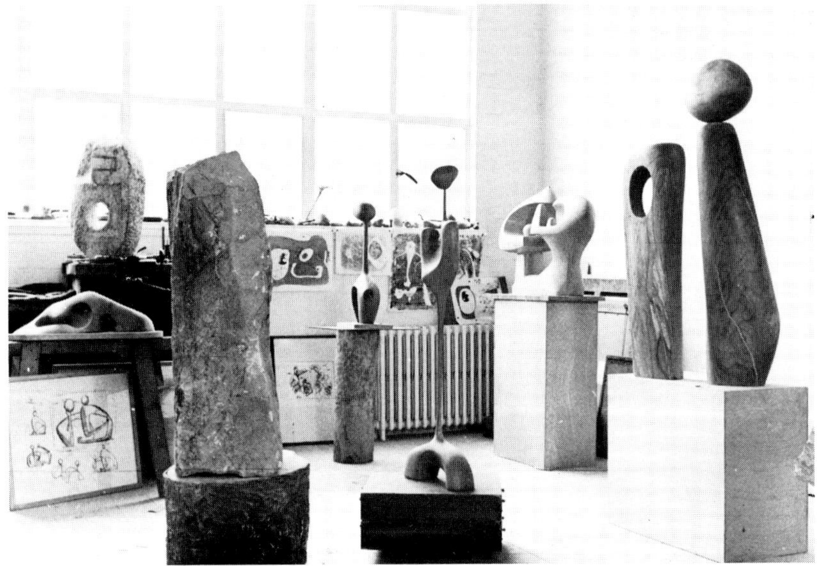

Studio, New Malden, 1939

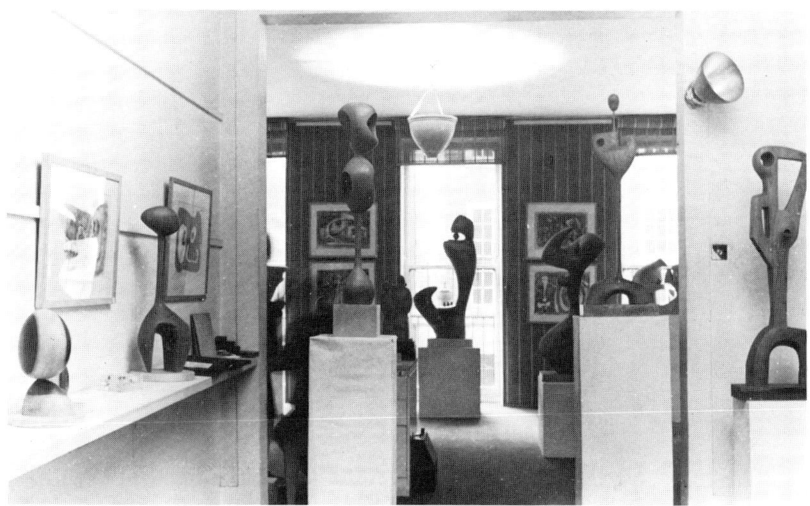

F. E. McWilliam exhibition at London Gallery, March, 1939

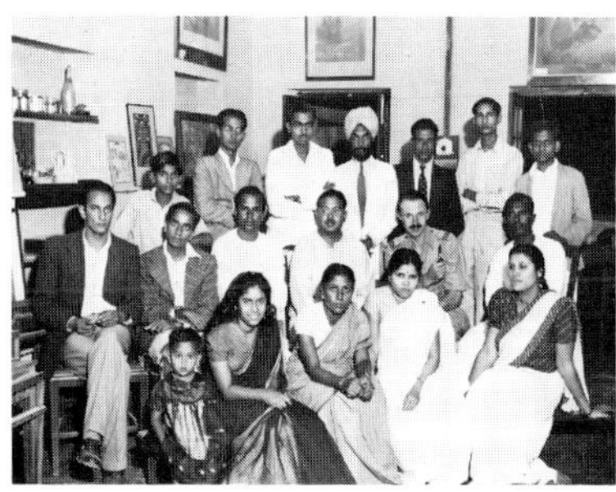

With Art School staff and students, New Delhi, 1945

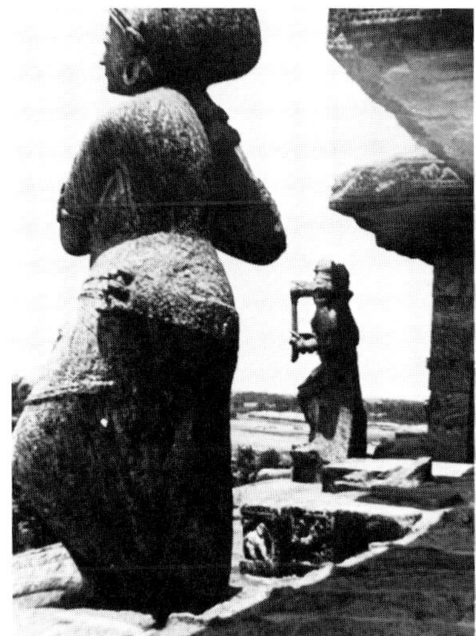

Hindu temple at Puri, Orissa (photo by McWilliam, 1945)

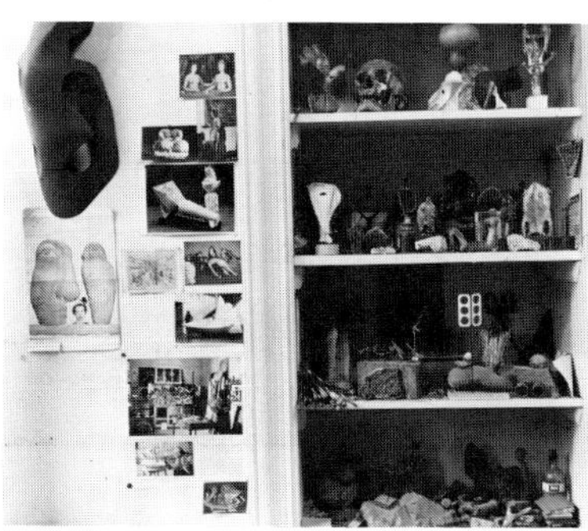

Studio, Holland Park, 1951

1944-46

Service in India. First in New Delhi, where he taught life drawing at the local Hindu Art School on an informal basis and introduced life drawing, and later in Bengal. Visited and photographed the Hindu temples at Puri, Orissa.

1946-47

Taught sculpture at Chelsea School of Art. Began friendship with Ceri and Frances Richards. Resumed sculpture in various materials, including terra-cotta, cast stone and concrete, as well as wood and stone (see 'The Long Arm' cat.20; 'Bengali Figure' cat.29 ; 'Kneeling Man' cat.31; 'Roman Matron' cat.32 etc.).

With friends Merlyn Evans, Charles Howard, McWilliam attended meetings of reconstituted Surrealist group at Barcelona Café, but Surrealism as an organised movement was no longer of any great interest to him.

1947

Appointed by A. H. Gerrard to teach sculpture at the Slade School, a post he retained until 1968. First commission, by Roland Penrose: 'Kneeling Woman').

In Paris, he visited Brancusi, whose work he had admired since first encountering it in *Cahiers d'Art* in the late '20s. Later he met Giacometti and Laurens.

1950s

Moved to studio house in Holland Park (1950).

At *Festival of Britain* exhibition he was commissioned to create large figurative work on subject of 'The Four Seasons' for the Country Pavilion on the South Bank. Also contributed to Festival *International Open Air Sculpture Exhibition* in Battersea Park.

Exhibiting regularly at the Hanover Gallery (1949/52/56), and in important group and survey shows, here and abroad.

Semi-abstract linear figures in bronze (see 'Eve' cat.37 ; 'Patriarch' cat.38; 'Man Erect' cat.39).

'Cain and Abel' maquette, submitted to the *Unknown Political Prisoner* competition exhibition in early 1953, was the first of McWilliam's works to be acquired by the Tate Gallery. Of its subject he wrote (May 1953): 'I took this as a symbol of man's eternal persecution of man, of which the political prisoner is but the contemporary symptom . . .'.

At this time he first met Eugene Rosenberg, the architect, who became a close friend of the artist, a major collector of his work, and was to be responsible for the commissioning of 'Princess Macha' 1957 (ill. p.20).

In 1959, despite never having submitted work for exhibition, McWilliam was appointed Associate of the Royal Academy, being proposed by Ruskin Spear. This ended his association with the Hanover Gallery, whose *avant-garde* credentials were compromised by his election. Though he met certain sympathetic individuals, notably Basil Spence the architect, which led to the commissions at Southampton ('Puy de Dome' 1962) and Hampstead ('Hampstead Figure' 1964: ill. p.21), McWilliam never felt at home at the R.A. In 1963, irritated by the Hanging Committee's rejection of a picture submitted for the Summer Exhibition by William Gear, whom he considered to be a painter at least as good as most academicians, he resigned from the Academy. At the same time he resigned from the London Group, to which he had been elected in 1949, asserting once and for all his determination to be free of group and institutional entanglements.

Complex semi-figurative bronzes; standing reliefs; 1957: 'Princess Macha' commissioned for Altnagelvin Hospital, Derry.

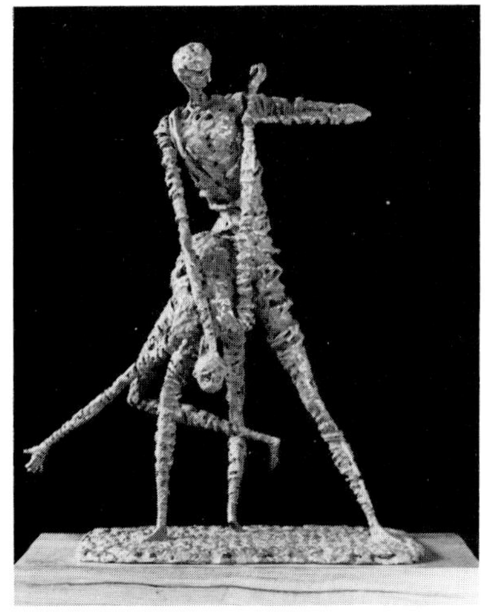

'Cain and Abel', 1953

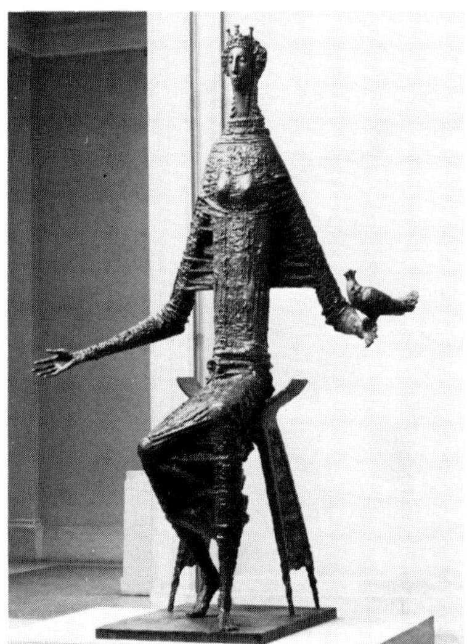

'Princess Macha' on exhibition at the Tate Gallery, 1957

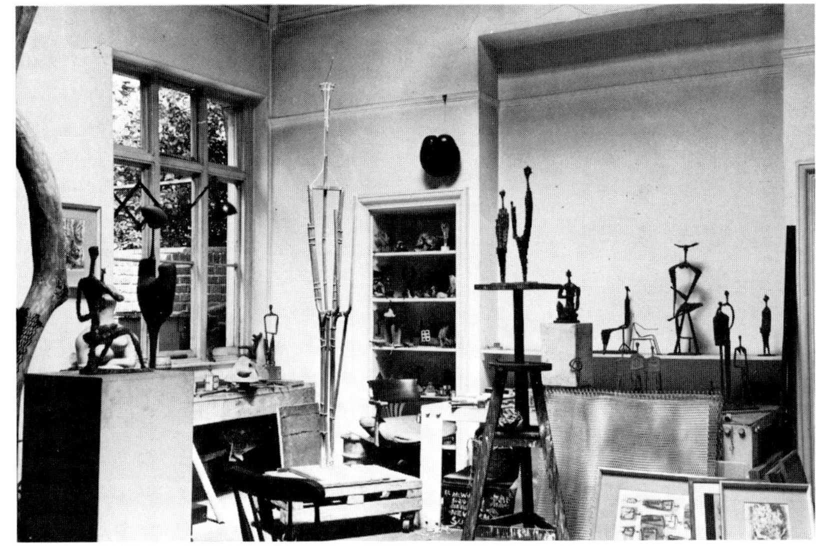

Studio, Holland Park, 1953. The 'Coco de mer ''bean'' ' is on the wall above the recess

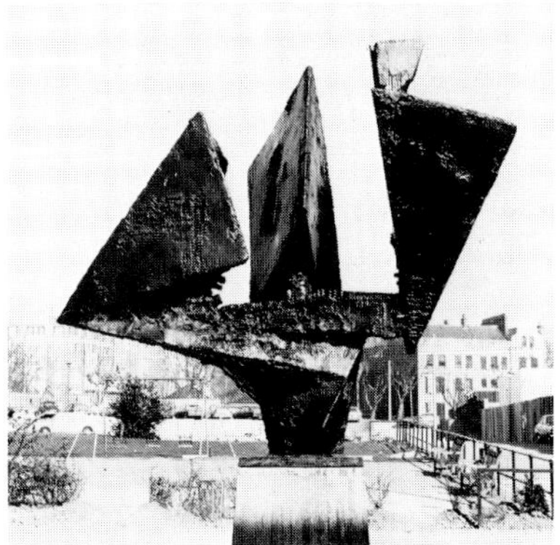

'Hampstead Figure', 1964

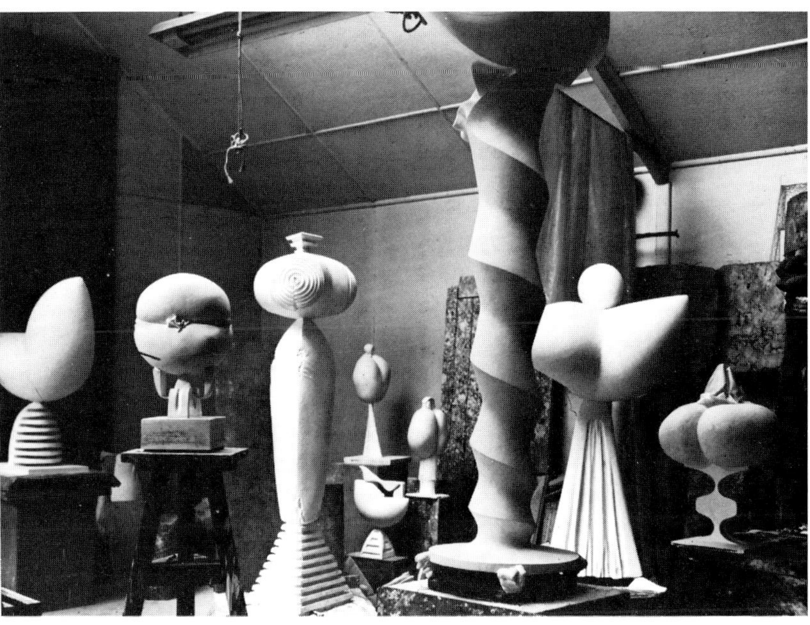

Work in progress, 'Bean' sculptures, Holland Park studio, 1965

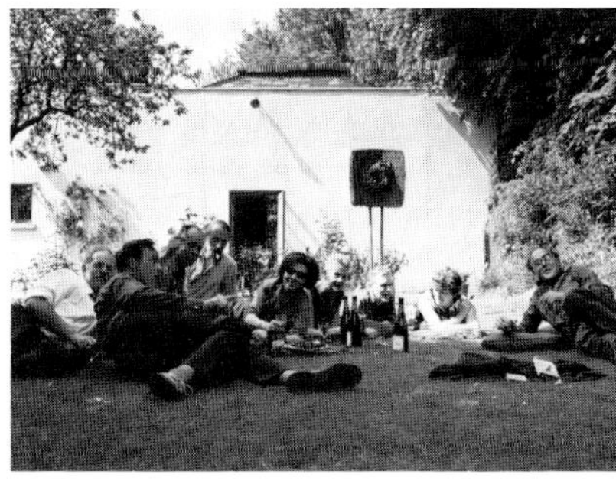

Party in Holland Park Garden following opening at Tate of 'Painting and Sculpture of a Decade 54/64', April 1964. Left to right: Terry Frost, Patrick Heron, Bryan Wynter, F. E. McWilliam, Mary Scott, Beth McWilliam, William Scott, Delia Heron, Roger Hilton (photo by McWilliam)

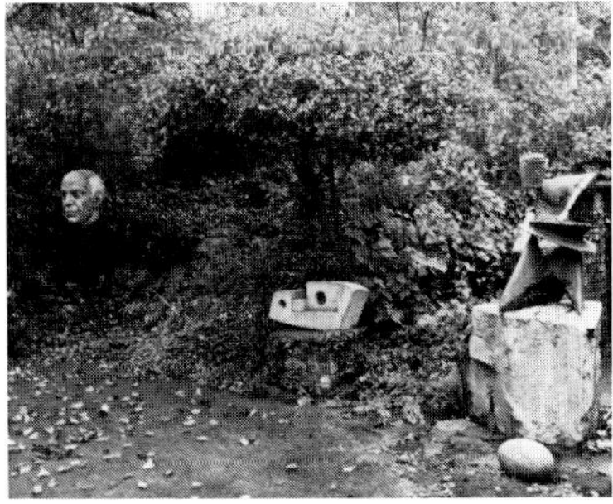

A corner of the garden, Holland Park, 1967, with 'Head of Picasso' 1967, 'Abstract Carving' 1938, and 'Figure with Hoops 1964

1960s/1970s/1980s

Continued to exhibit regularly, at the Waddington Galleries in London, and in major survey shows here and abroad.

1962-64: Bronze horizontal figures (see cat.41-47 inclusive). 1965-66: Bronze Bean sculptures (see cat.50-55 inclusive).

In 1963 he fulfilled a long-held ambition to travel to Greece. The experience confirmed his deep sympathies with things Mediterranean and classical, sympathies 'tempered with a touch of irrational Gothic'.

In 1964 his friend Roland Penrose concluded his introduction of a comprehensive photographic survey of his work with the words: 'McWilliam is an inventor of styles. The variety we see in his work is a symptom of his restless enquiry into the substance of living things, into their movement their meetings, their separations and the flow of life in their veins. He has the capacity to relate our daily existence with existence which is fundamental and timeless. He has above all the understanding and the instincts of a poet'.

Late 60s: After a visit to Mexico he experimented with fibre-glass with mosaic facing. Most successful of these works is 'Head of Picasso' 1967. 1969-70: Bronze 'Girls', part modelled, part shiny-faceted.

1964: Honorary D.Litt., Queen's University, Belfast.

1966: C.B.E.

1971: Oireachtas Gold Medal, Trinity College, Dublin.

In 1972/3 Bronze 'Women of Belfast' series: outraged by the bombing of the Abercorn Tea Rooms in Belfast, McWilliam made a series of figurative sculptures depicting women caught in the blast: 'These sculptures are concerned with violence, with one particular aspect, bomb-blast – the women as victims of man's stupidity'.

1975-77: Bronze 'Banners'.

1977-81: Bronze 'Legs' (see cat.57-69 inclusive).

1983-89: Begins carving in wood again (see cat.72-85 inclusive).

April 1988 Death of Beth McWilliam.

During the great storm of October 1987 an ancient mulberry tree in the artist's garden was uprooted. The wood from this casualty provided McWilliam with the material and the inspiration for his latest series of sculptures, the 'Mulberry Family' of 1988/89 (see cat.78-85 inclusive). Work on this series continues.

Note: Unless otherwise stated, all quotations are from the artist. Acknowledgements are due to Judy Marle, T. P. Flanagan and Louisa Buck.

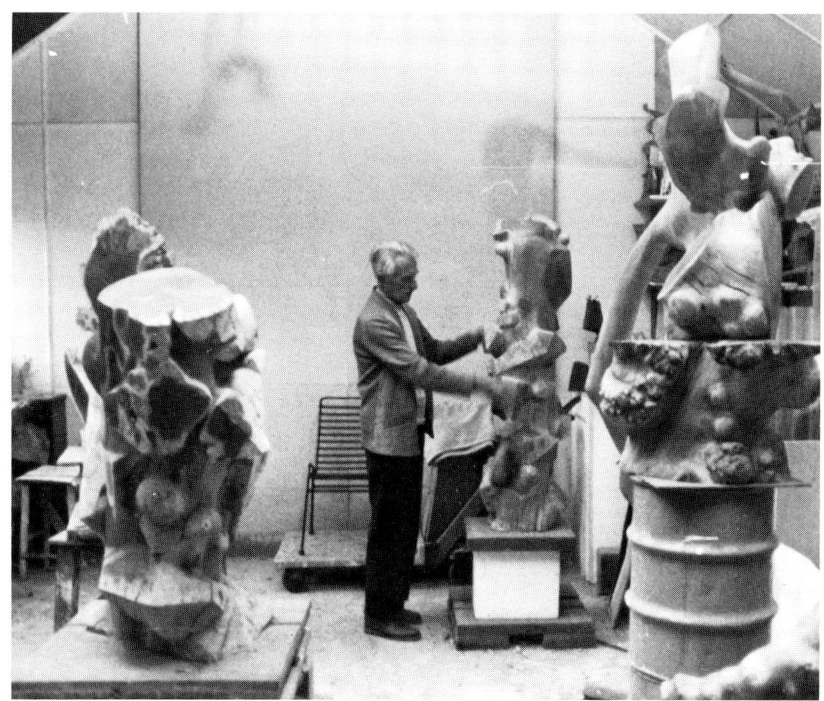

Work in progress, 'Mulberry Figures', Holland Park studio, 1989

Notes to the Introduction and Chronology

Quotations from F. E. McWilliam are drawn from interviews with the artist by T. P. Flanagan and Judy Marle (quoted in *F. E. McWilliam*, Ulster Museum catalogue, April 1981); Mel Gooding (*Arts Review*, November 1981); Bryan Robertson (Introduction to *F. E. McWilliam: Early Sculptures 1935-48 with some recent works*, Warwick Arts Trust 1982); and from McWilliam's introductory note to the *Women of Belfast* exhibition at McClelland International Gallery, Belfast, in 1973.

Other sources quoted are as follows:

Roland Penrose, *McWilliam*, Alec Tiranti, London, 1964

John Fowles, *The French Lieutenant's Woman*, Jonathan Cape, London, 1969 (Chapter 13)

Henry Moore, Notes on Sculpture in *The Painter's Object*, ed. Myfanwy Evans, Gerald Howe, London, 1937

Carola Giedion-Welcker, *Constantin Brancusi*, Editions du Griffon, Neuchâtel, Switzerland, 1959

Adrian Stokes, *The Stones of Rimini*, Faber and Faber, London, 1934

Herbert Read, *Henry Moore Sculptor, An Appreciation*, A. Zwemmer, London, 1934

Luis Buñuel, *My Last Breath*, Jonathan Cape, London, 1984

Igor Stravinsky, *Poetics of Music. In the form of six lessons*, Harvard University Press, Cambridge, Massachusetts, 1942 (Lesson 3 'The Composition of Music')

A Note on the Selection

This retrospective selection of work by F. E. McWilliam makes no claim to be comprehensive: it reflects an individual response to the extraordinary range and variety of the artist's work, and a particular critical determination. This was to display as far as possible within the scale of the exhibition the diversity of subject matter and technique that has marked McWilliam's output, and at the same time highlight particular themes and present them in depth. McWilliam has always tended to work in series, taking an idea and exploring it exhaustively before moving on to something different: the exhibition has been selected and arranged to reflect that characteristic procedure. To do this has required the exclusion of a great many works that would be necessary to a retrospective claiming completeness of representation. It means also that it is possible to envisage a quite different exhibition, equally selective, making other emphases, presenting another image of the work.

Such an exhibition might place a greater emphasis upon the mythic and hieratic themes and iconography of the 'fifties, that considerable body of work, figurative and abstract, that put McWilliam in the mainstream of post-war expressive sculpture. It would certainly include the series of powerful 'Heads' of 1960, which match the originality of Moore's 'Helmet Heads' in conception, but are more organic, less schematically armour-like. And it would find space for the dynamic semi-figurative bronze works of 1961 and 1962. This rich decade of often troubled and troubling imagery is represented in the present exhibition by three works which seem to emerge from its *furore* as images of majestic calm and clarity: 'Eve' and 'Patriarch' of 1953, and 'Ikon' of 1960. I would have also liked to include 'Princess Macha' of 1957, which seems to me to occupy a special place in McWilliam's *oeuvre*. From this period, there is also the in some ways untypical 'Man Erect' of 1955. From the later 'sixties and the 'seventies this other exhibition would show, perhaps, certain of the works in which McWilliam experimented with coloured mosaic (experiment which the artist, incidentally, regards as largely unsuccessful, though it produced the remarkable likeness of 'Head of Picasso' in 1967). It would include the 'Girls' of 1969-71, whose images are partly modelled, partly incised into the shiny flat planes created by slicing away sections of the three-dimensional forms. It would recognise the significance, and the artistic bravery, of the violently kinetic 'Women of Belfast' series of 1972-75, in which virtuosity is placed at the service of a direct moral engagement.

McWilliam's work, in all its moods and diversities of form and medium, has from the beginning been characterised by witty and fantastic invention. The artist is known for his wilful shifts of mode, his inveterate tendency to do the unexpected thing, his disregard for aesthetic convention, his love of the caprice and of the visual and verbal joke, his *insouciant* individuality: the sterner criticism which looks for programme and 'development' has been disconcerted by these things. McWilliam's greatest consistency has been in his capacity to surprise, to take a convention and subvert it to satiric or celebratory purposes. It is not surprising that among his greatest admirers have been fellow artists, especially those affected by the spirit of surrealism: Henry Moore, Paul Nash, E. L. T. Mesens, Roland Penrose, Ceri Richards, Merlyn Evans, T. P. Flanagan. Such kindred spirits know that art works as a form of magic, a kind of wisdom that finds truth in the unexpected and the unpredictable; that the first rule of art is to break rules and rediscover living meanings behind custom and convention.

The selection I have made for this exhibition has tended to emphasise those aspects of McWilliam's output in which his predisposition to the metamorphic and the fantastic has been given fullest expression. This accords with my view that it is in the persistent recurrence throughout his career of a transformative surreality that we find his most original and distinctive contribution to the art of our century. In making it I have enjoyed the closest collaboration with the artist, whose help has been of inestimable value.

To work with Mac has been a rare privilege; it does not extend, however, to protect me from the critical consequences of a choice of emphasis and of works that is my responsibility alone.

Mel Gooding, January 1989

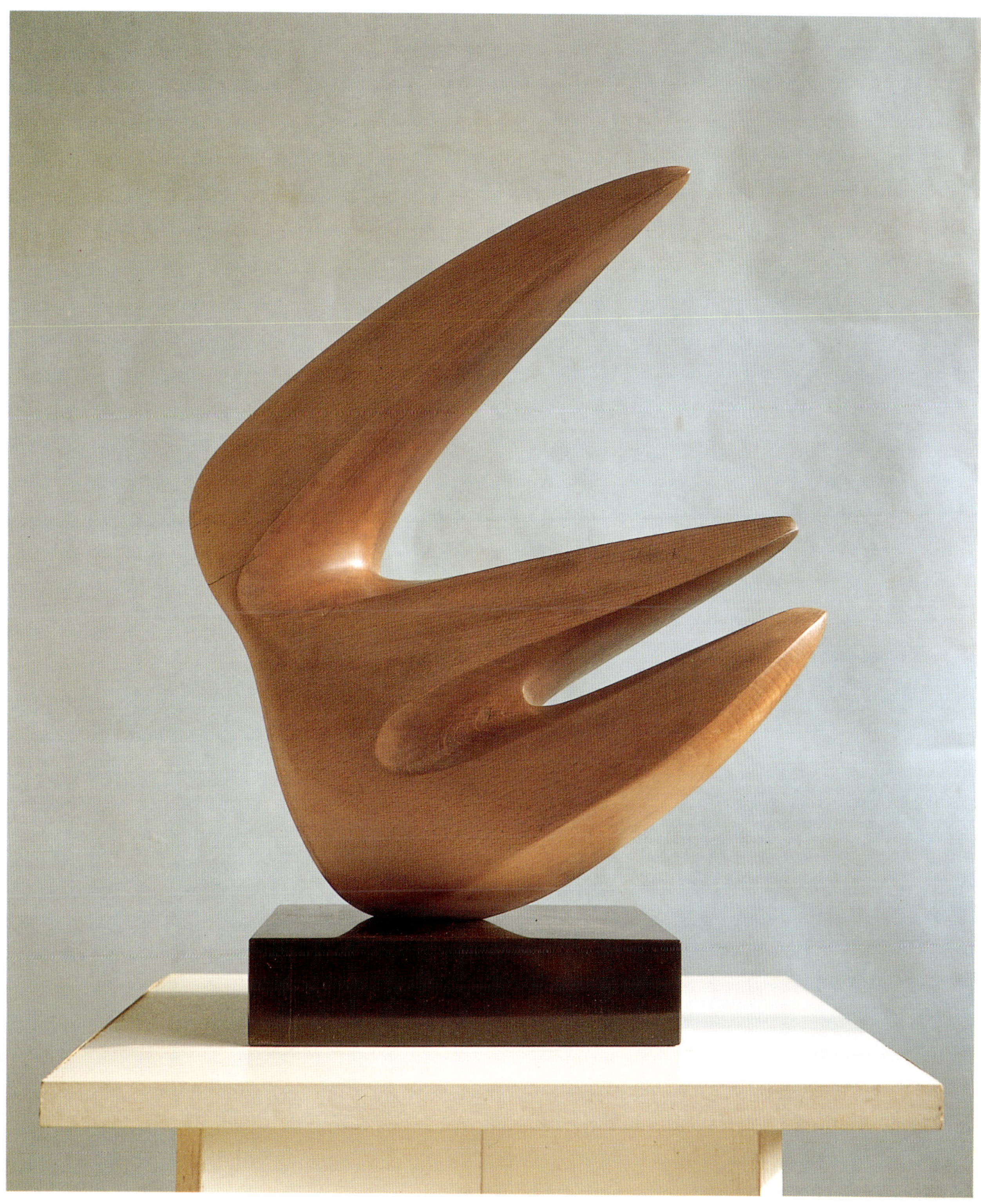

Three Prongs 1935 (9)

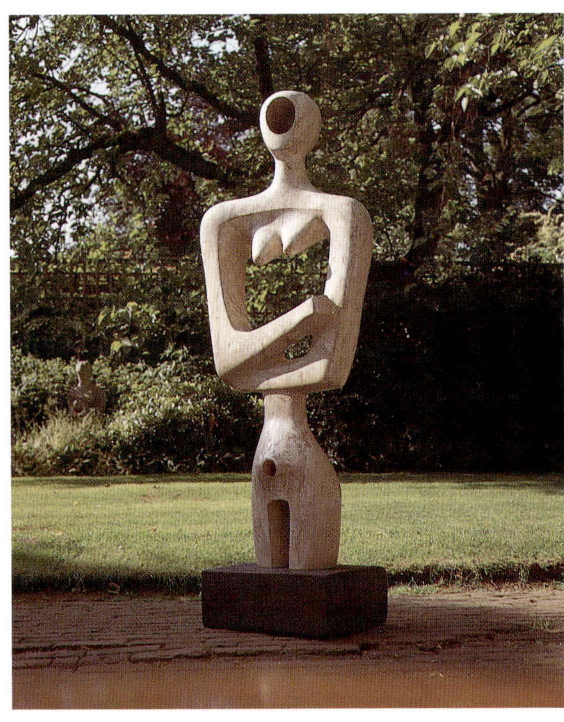

Hollow Figure 1936 (14)

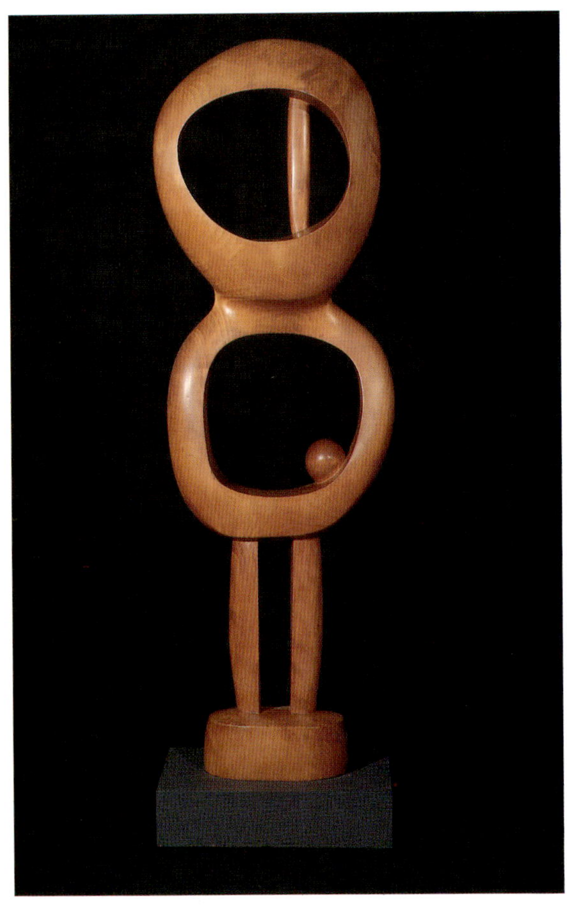

Figure 1937 (16)

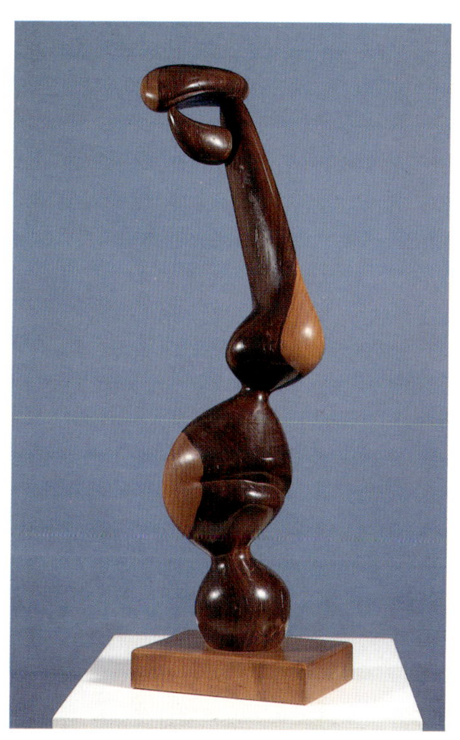

Profile 1939-40 (19)

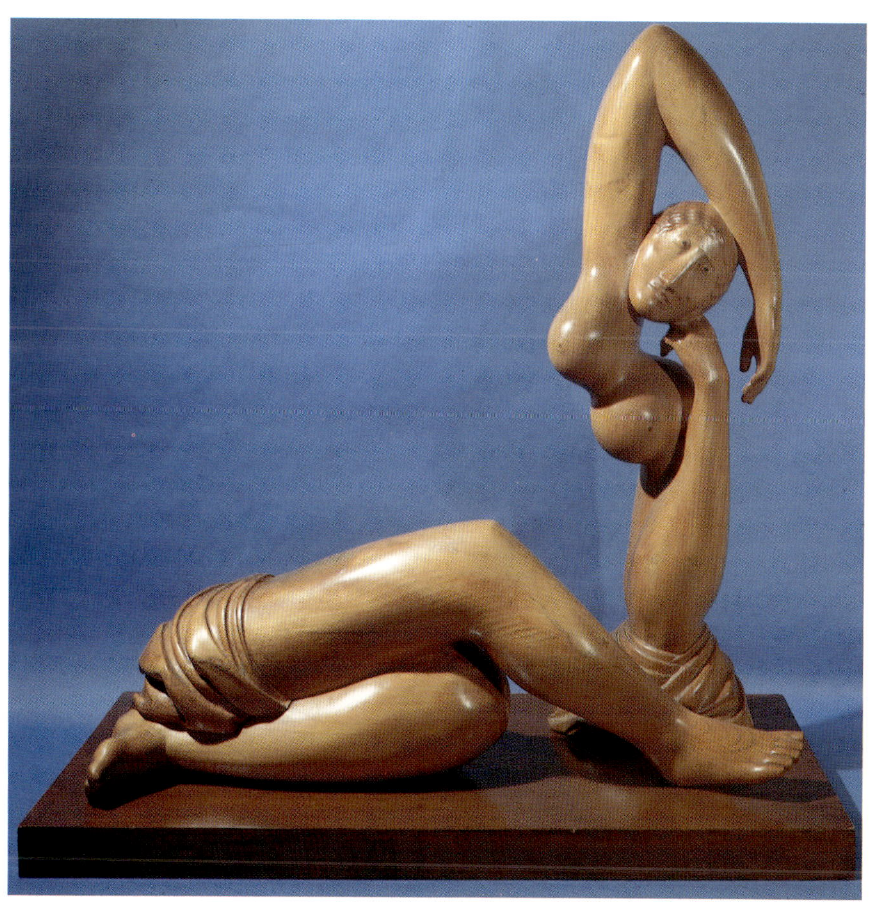

Roman Matron 1948 (32)

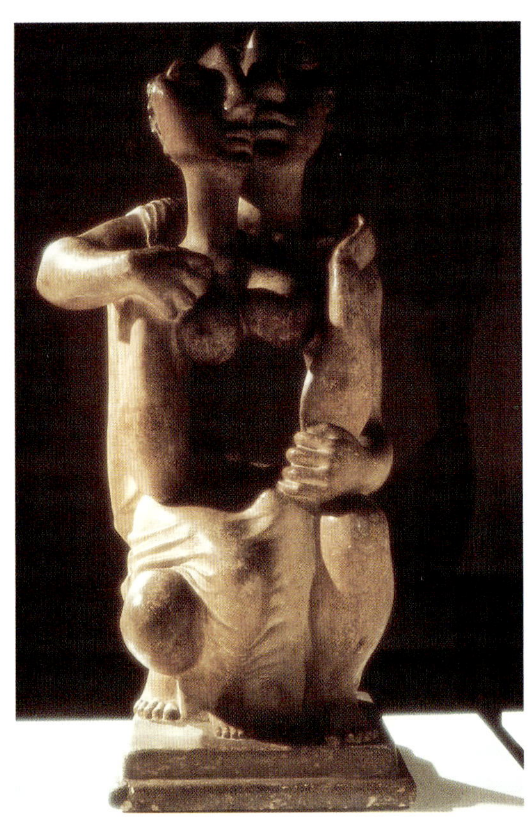

Man and Wife 1948 (34)

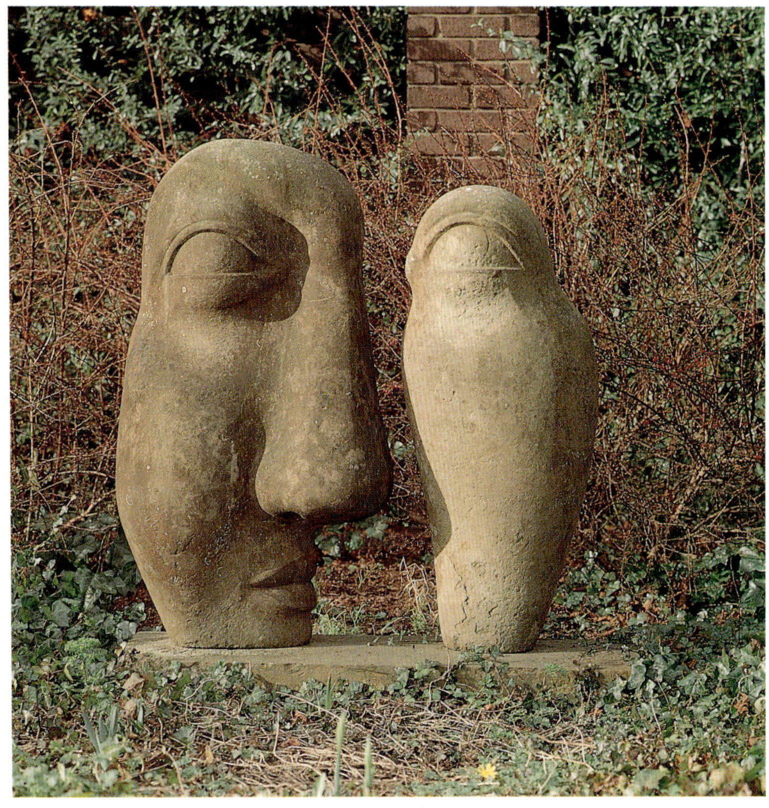

Irish Head 1949 (36)

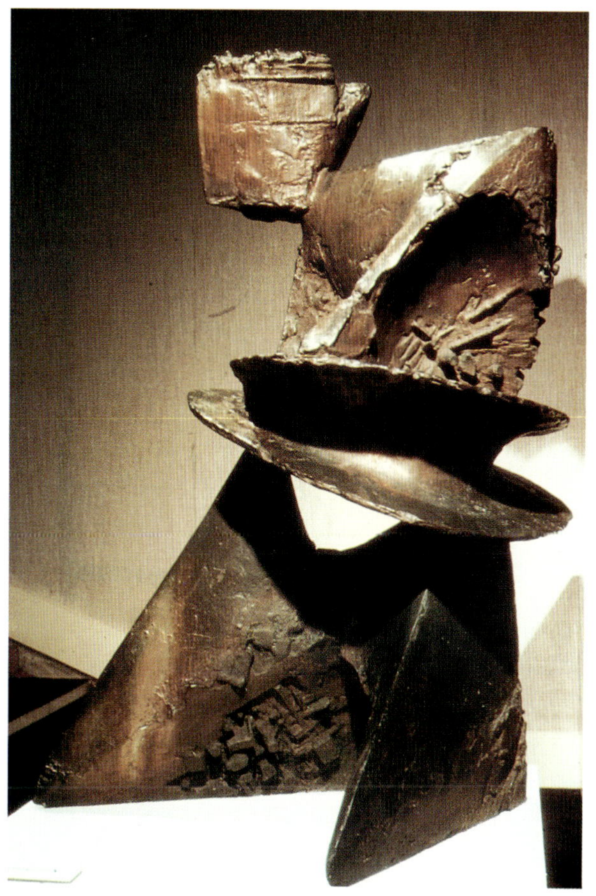

Figures with Hoops 1964 (48)

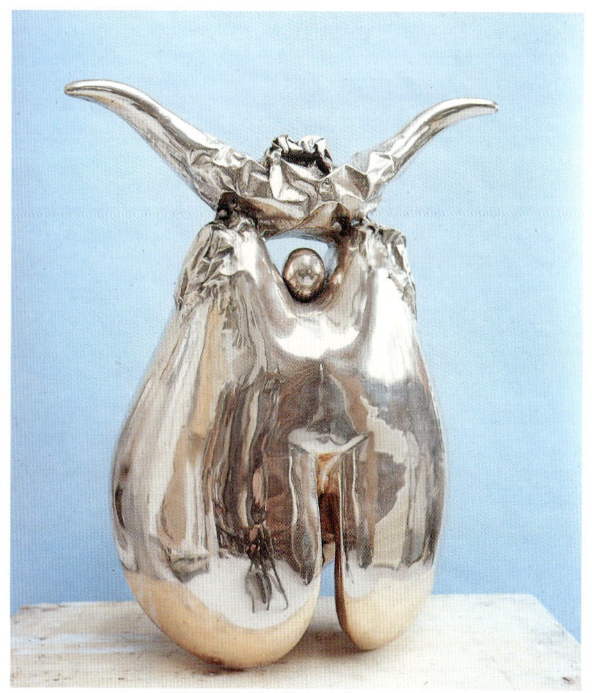

Nordic Bean 1965 (50)

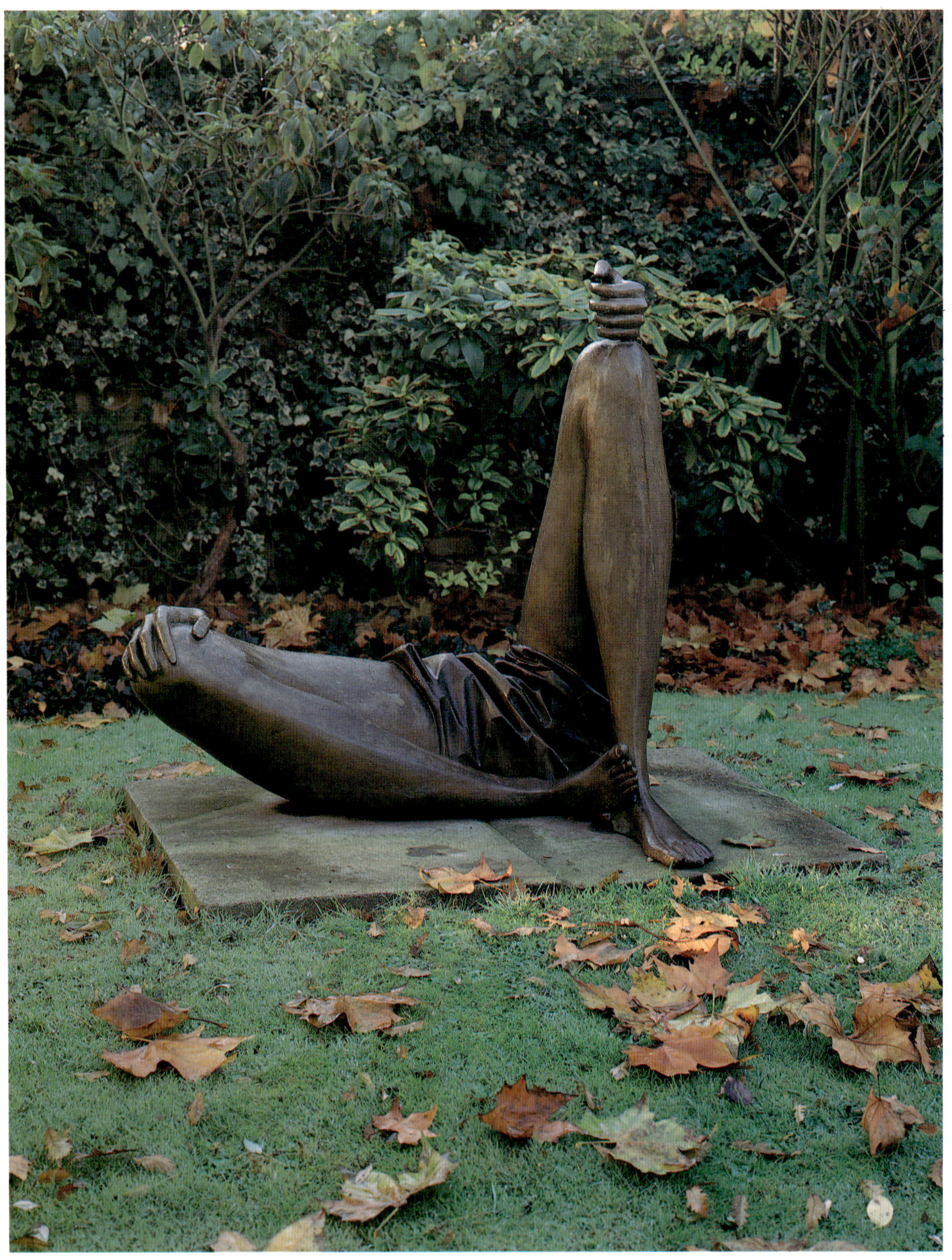

Legs Static 1978 (61)

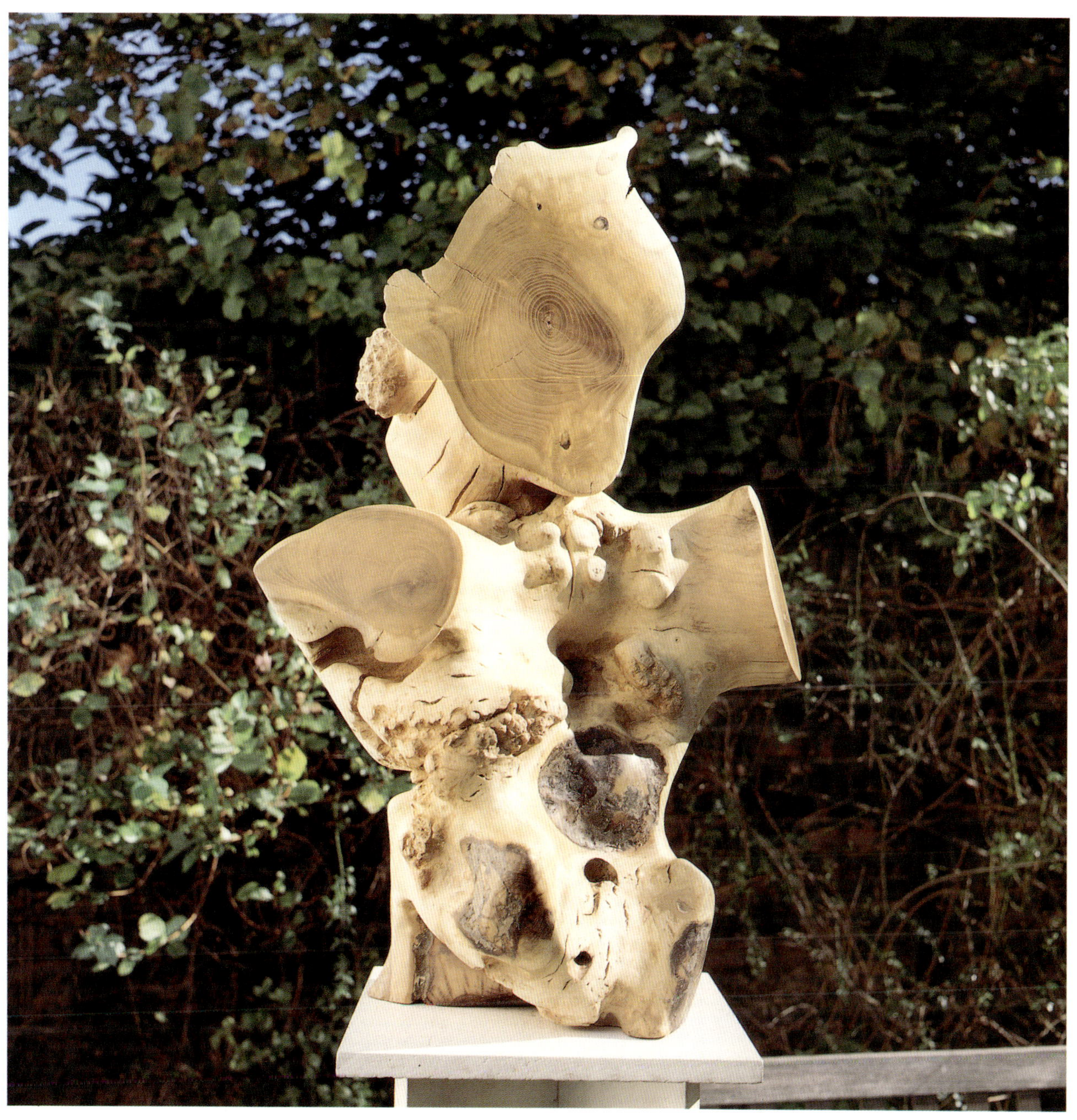

Mulberry Figure Six 1988 (83)

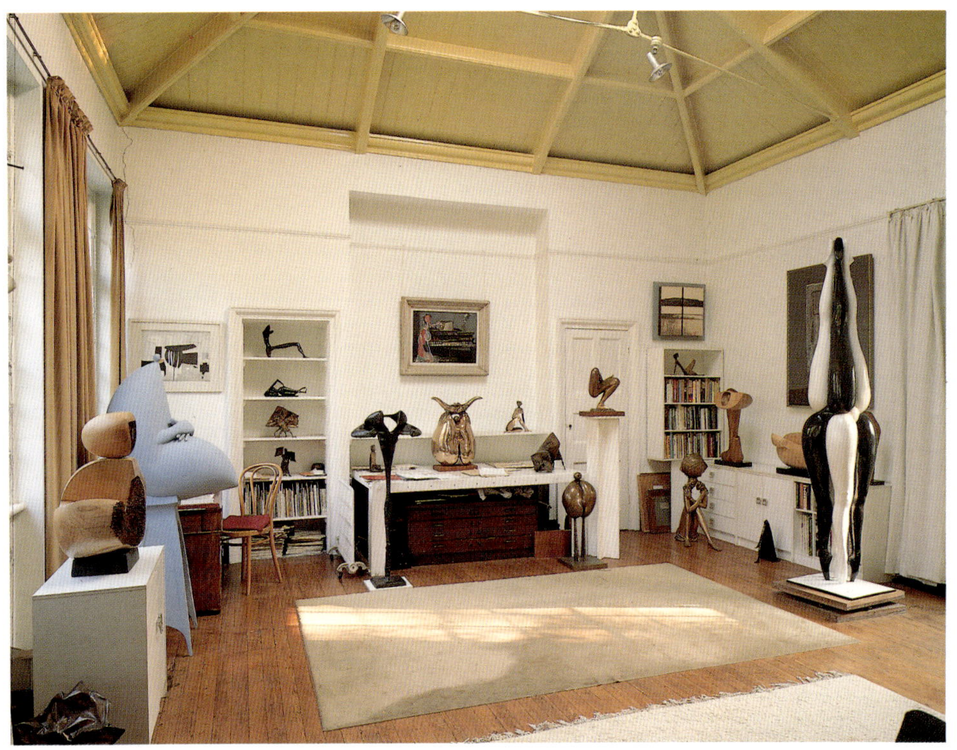

The Artist's Sitting Room, 1988

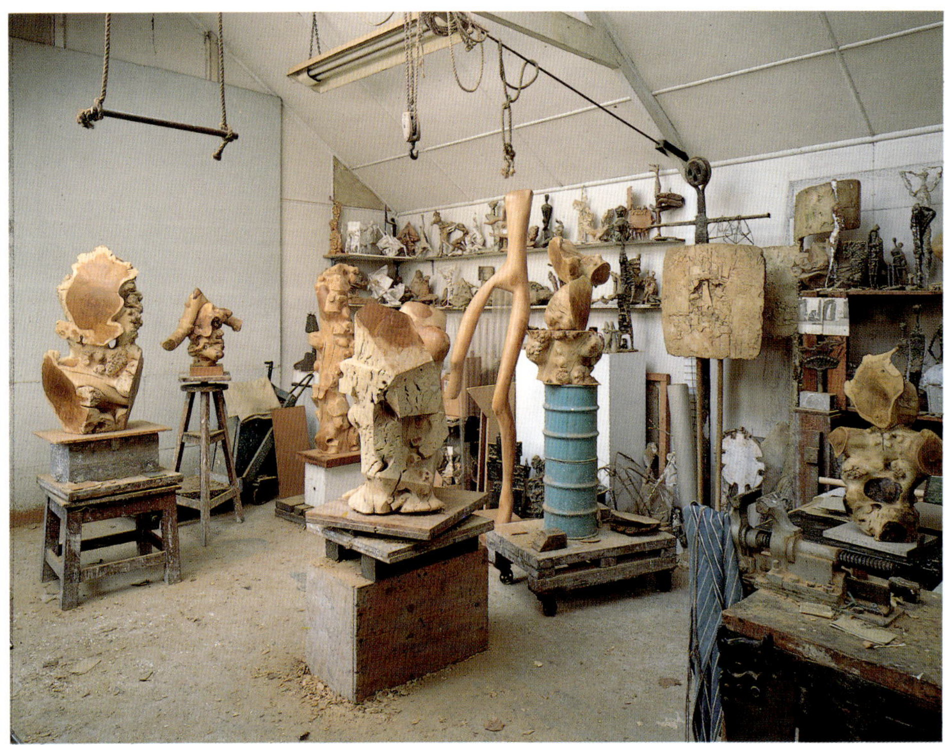

The Artist's Studio, 1988

[32]

Catalogue

For the sizes either height (h.) or length (l.) is
given indicating the greatest dimension. Inches precede
centimetres, which are given in brackets.

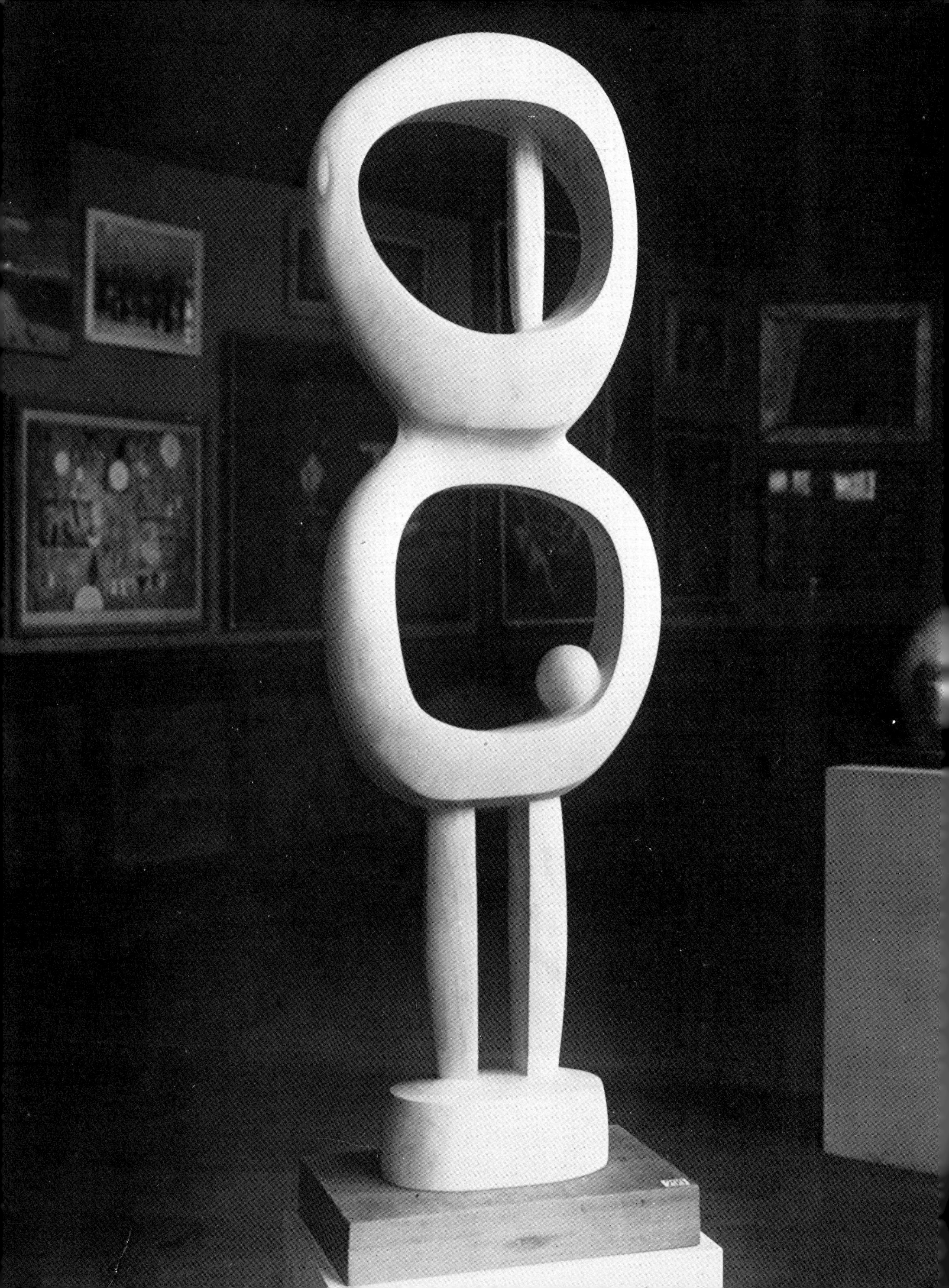

I Wood Carvings 1932-1939

McWilliam began in earnest to carve in wood upon his return from France in 1932. An awareness of the plastic vitality and emotive force of the forms of African sculpture had been a dynamic factor in the development of both French and German painting and sculpture during the first great period of Modernism. Later on, in the 'twenties and 'thirties, surrealism had stressed the archetypal resonance of primitive imagery, and recognised the psychic power of fetish objects. Although he was working at first in comparative isolation, McWilliam was clearly aware of the sculptural possibilities presented by the example of primitive and archaic carving and object making, as well as of the classical; nobody seriously interested in the art at that time could fail to be. (In Paris he had spent far more time looking at African sculpture in the ethnographic Musée de l'Homme than at the Louvre.) But his use of those sources was to be somewhat personal and oblique. Epstein was an early hero, and from Moore he 'caught the habit of visiting the British Museum and studying other cultures'. But, unlike either of his greatest contemporaries in this country, McWilliam was not interested in the monumental gravity suggested by certain archaic sculptural models.

'Mother and Child' (cat.1), the earliest work in the exhibition, demonstrates clearly his interest in African art, and his ability to make a modern work of great power and dignity drawing upon its forms and features. Even so, in its square-based solidity, its structural density, and its unambiguous statement of its theme, it remains unusual, and gives little hint of the direction McWilliam was to take.

'African Figure' (cat.2), made shortly after, whilst retaining the suggestion of an ethnic inspiration in the mask-like head, its frontality and its idol-like presence, signals a decisive shift towards more open forms, more ambiguous propositions. McWilliam, remarkably quickly, was establishing his own manner. At the heart of his approach, and this holds true for everything that he has made since, there is a dynamic aesthetic tension. On the one hand there is the impulse of the work to self-sufficient sculptural form, which might emerge variously as now more abstract, now more figurative; on the other an evocative allusiveness, a tendency to poetic reference to physiological and psychological human actualities, and by implication to matters emotional, sexual, political, or spiritual. The mood may be changeable, by turns ironic, celebratory, portentous, comic or violent, or multivalently any of these at once.

Brancusi's pure reduction of human forms was influential at this time (cat.8), and in Arp's pure-form *Torsos* of the early 'thirties McWilliam discovered a congruence of intention: 'Black Torso' (cat.7) was made, in fact, before he had actually seen those works. Biomorphic abstraction was very much in the air. McWilliam's carvings of this period are remarkable for their inventive variations on that theme, and their extension to it of an enigmatic and sometimes vaguely threatening aspect (cat.6; 9; 12; 13). The fetish, the idol, and their combination in the surreal *personnage* are other themes that McWilliam explored at this time, themes to which he was to return persistently in his future career (cat. 3; 5; 10; 14; 15; 16; 17; 18). In several of these he adopted another characteristic device, and one which constitutes perhaps his most individual and singular invention: the adumbration of the figure by the depiction of limbs enclosing a space where the trunk of the body might be. This elimination of the torso wittily inverts what could be regarded as the major sculptural discovery of Rodin, the great father figure of modern sculpture, that the torso fragment could expressively represent the whole human form. More than that, it irreverently subverts a central premise of all classical and archaic sculpture, that its formal definition is physical mass.

With 'Profile' (cat. 19) and 'The Long Arm' (cat. 20) McWilliam carries to extremes another recurrent idea at odds with the formal tradition of sculpture as body and mass with a centre of gravity: that of attenuation and balance upon a narrow base. 'Profile' defies the convention of the head as a solid globe (a joke with Brancusi); 'The Long Arm' was paradoxically inspired by the monumental Egyptian fragment arm, long since 'horizontal', in the British Museum.

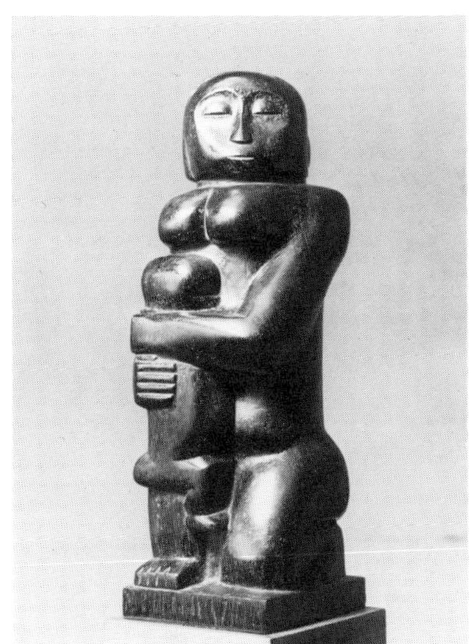

1 **Mother and Child** 1932/3
Teak h.19½ (49)
Private Collection

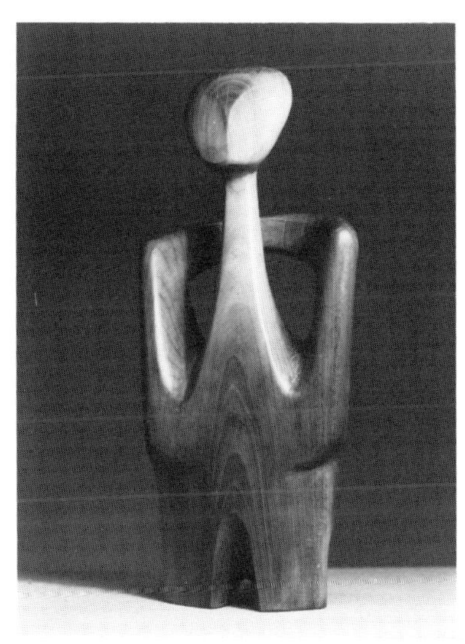

2 **African Figure** 1933
Cherry h.18 (46)
Janine Rensch, Switzerland

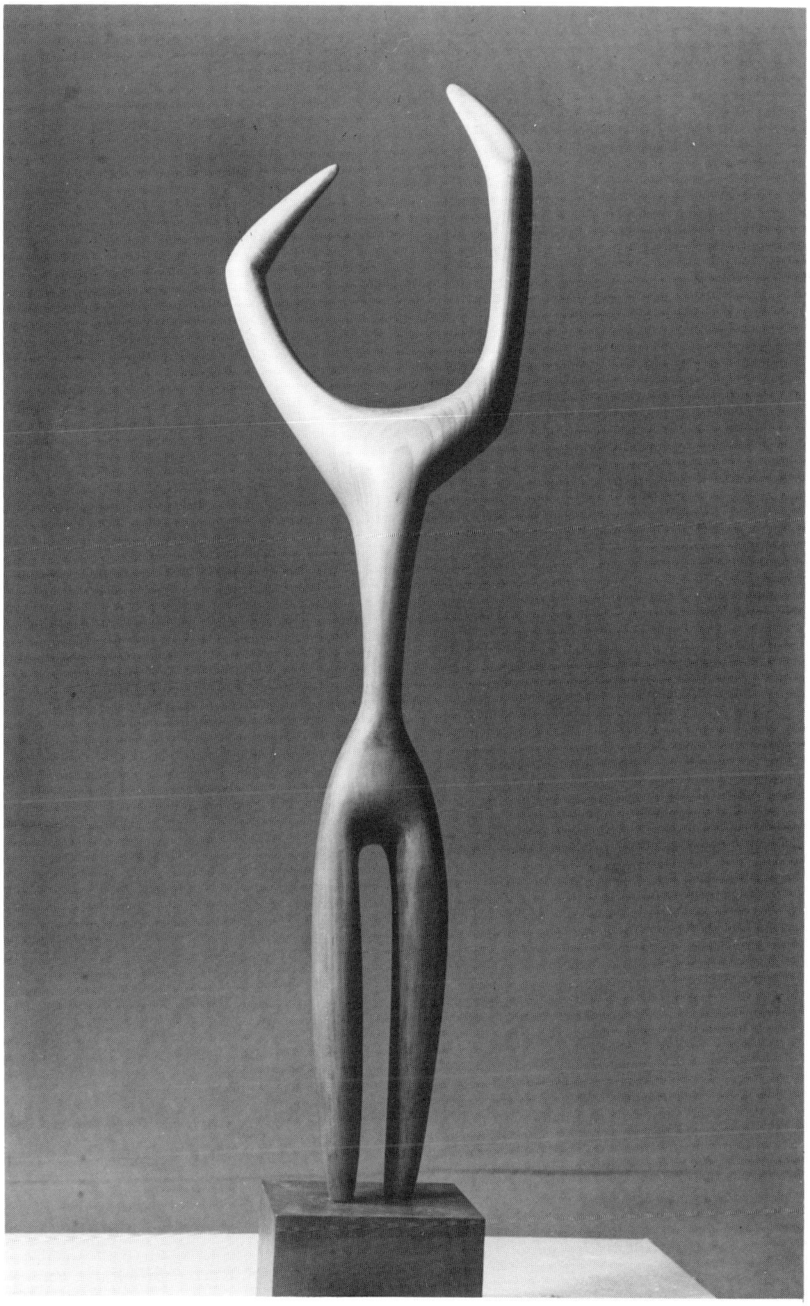

3 **Figure** 1933
Cherry h.43 (109)
Private Collection

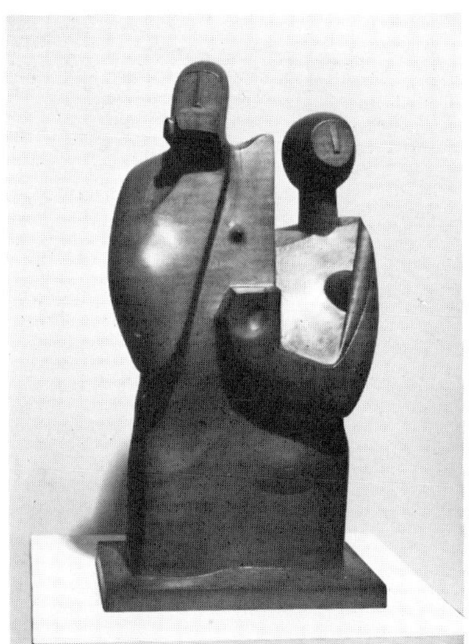

4 Man and wife 1934
Sycamore h.16½ (42)
George and Maura McClelland

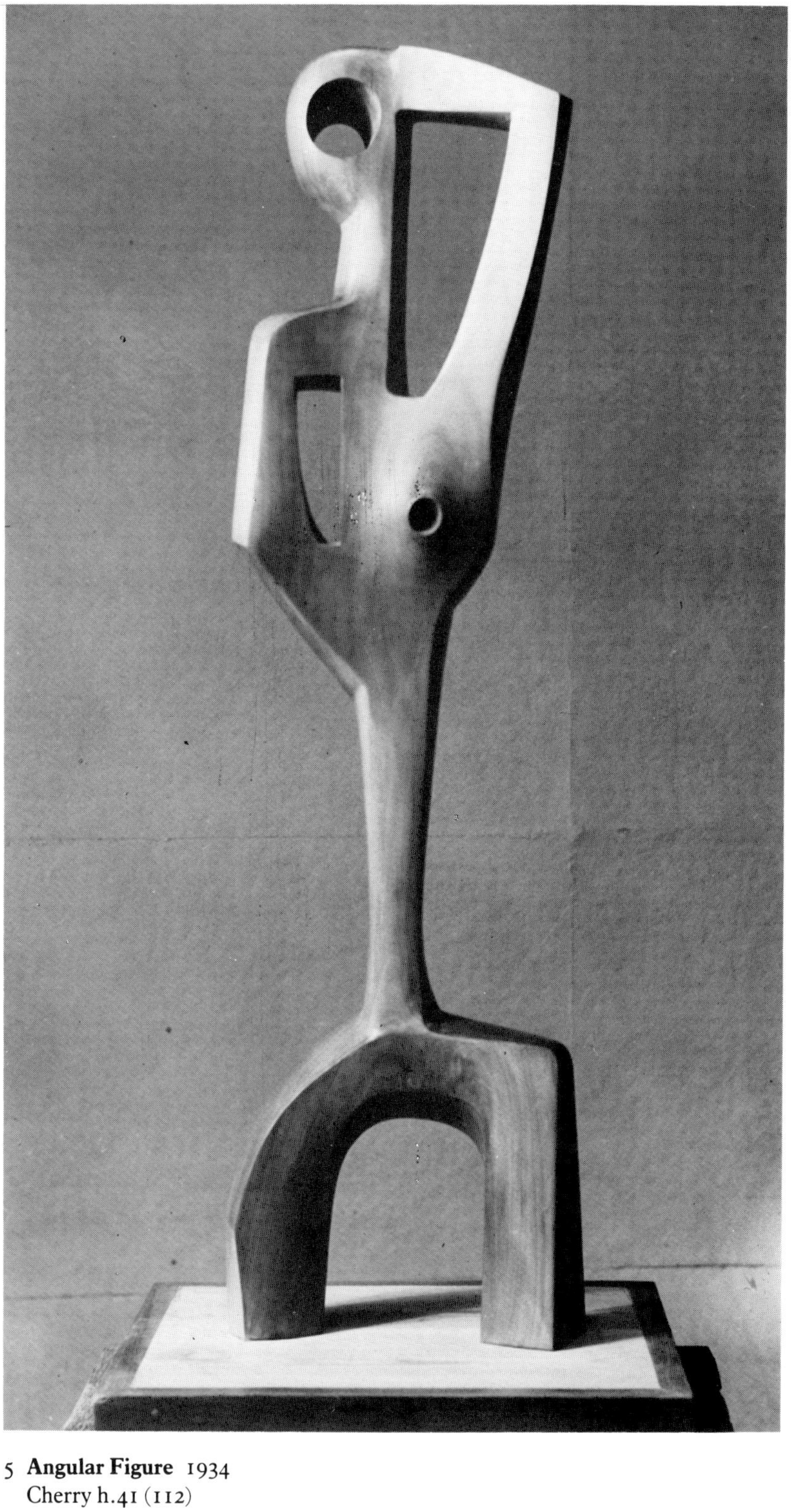

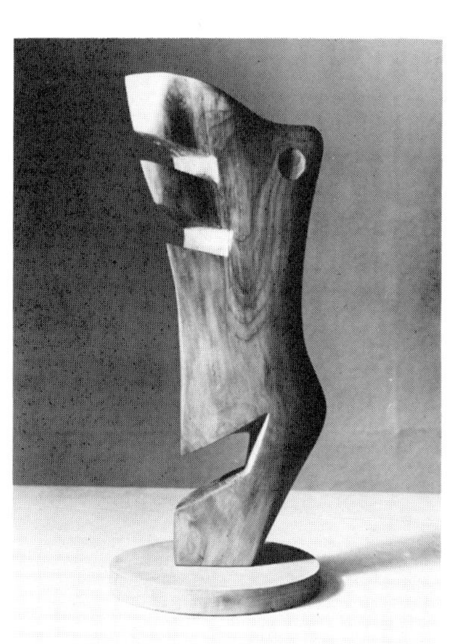

6 Axehead 1935 (renovated 1982)
Cherry h.22 (56)
*The Artist courtesy of the Mayor
Gallery*

5 Angular Figure 1934
Cherry h.41 (112)
*The Artist courtesy of the Albemarle
Gallery*

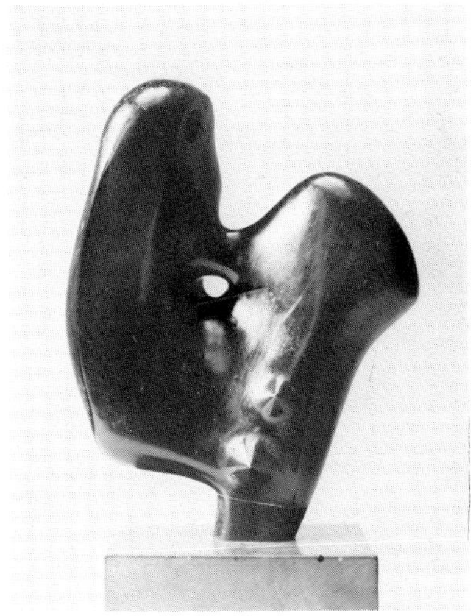

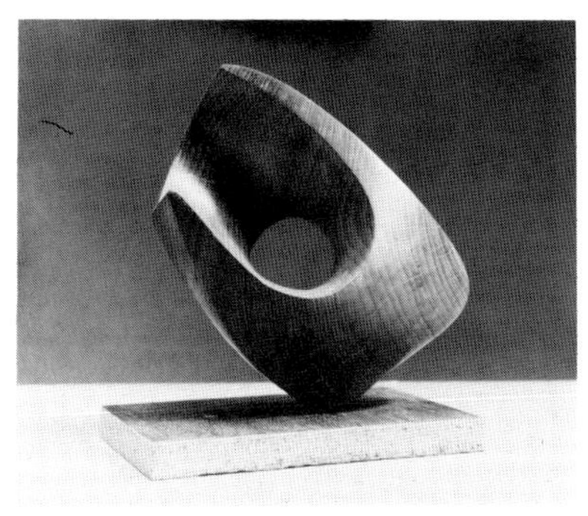

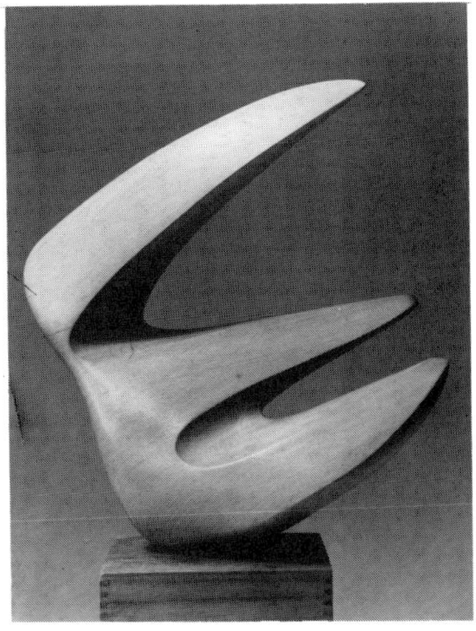

7 **Black Torso** 1935
Ebonised hardwood h.16½ (42)
The Artist

8 **Cave** 1935 (renovated 1982)
Beech h.8 (20)
Dr Terry Friedman

9 **Three Prongs** 1935
Beech h.16½ (42)
*Bradford Art Galleries and
Museums*

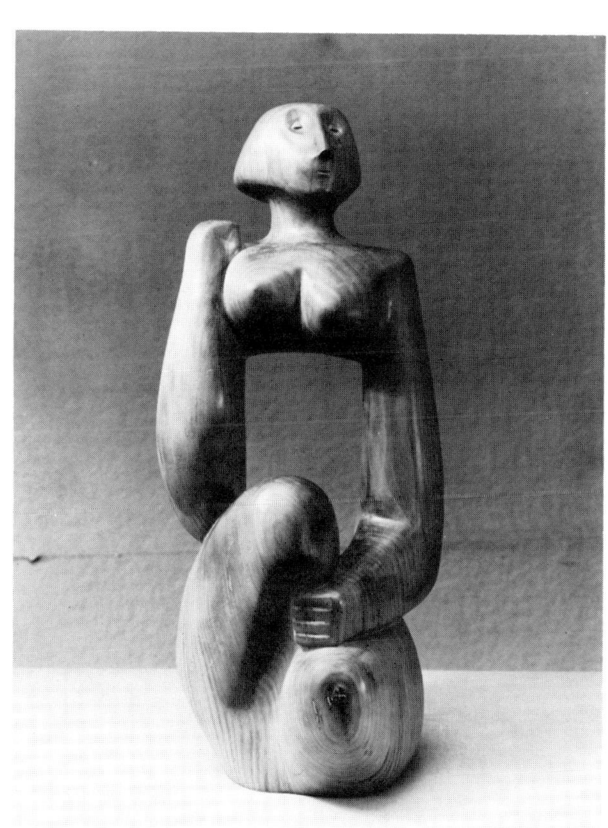

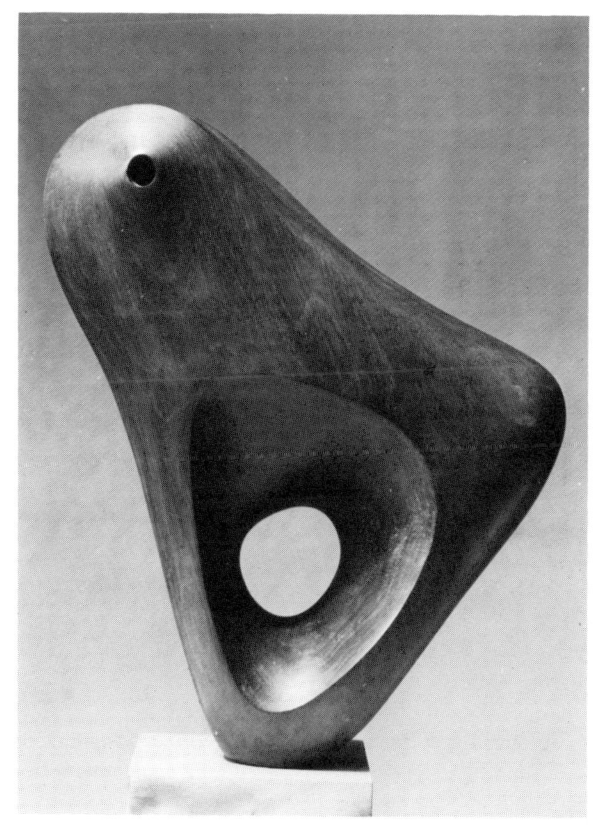

10 **Matriarch** 1935 (renovated 1984)
Cherry h.22 (56)
George and Maura McClelland

11 **Carving** 1936 (renovated 1984)
Walnut h.12½ (32)
Private Collection

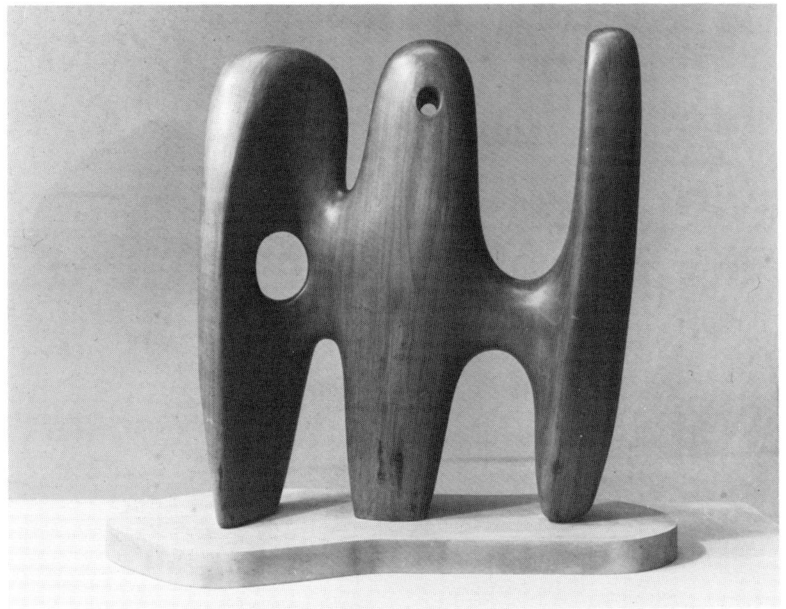

12 Trio 1936
Cherry h.18 (46)
Bridget John

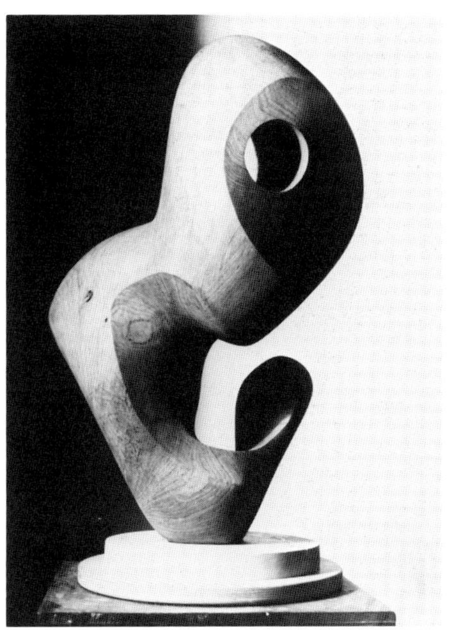

13 Carving 1936
Elm h.24 (61)
Private Collection

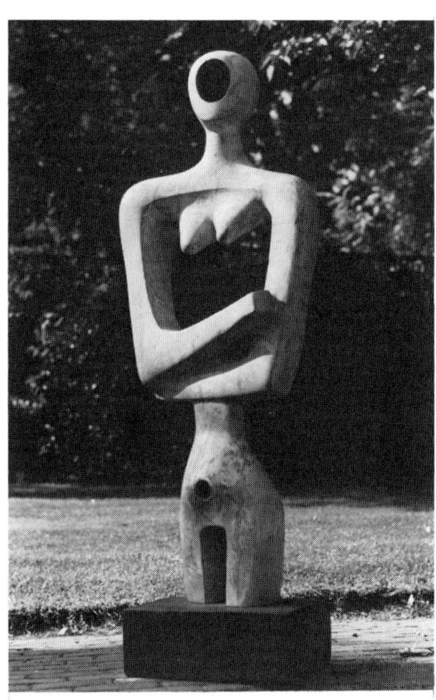

14 Hollow Figure 1936
Beech h.43½ (110)
John Evans

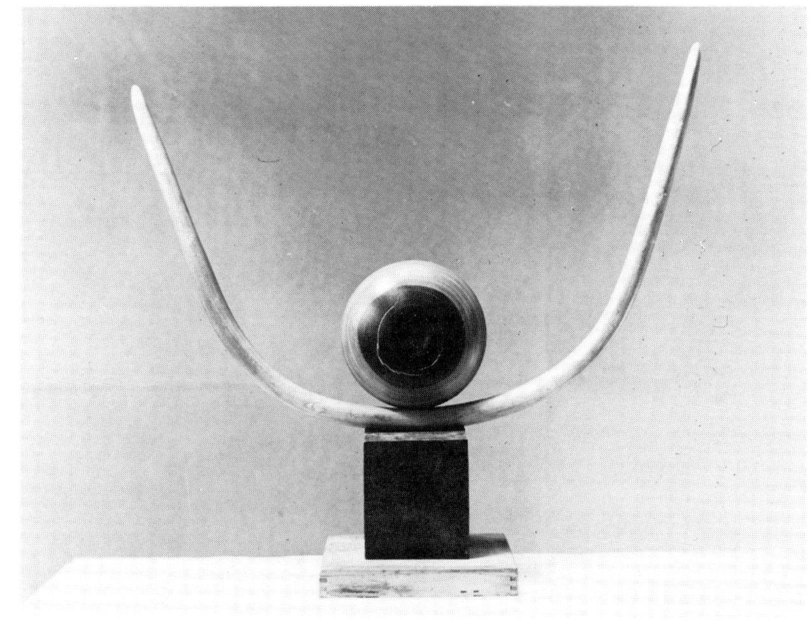

15 Oracle 1936
Lignum, vitae and beech l.20 (51)
Jessica Murray

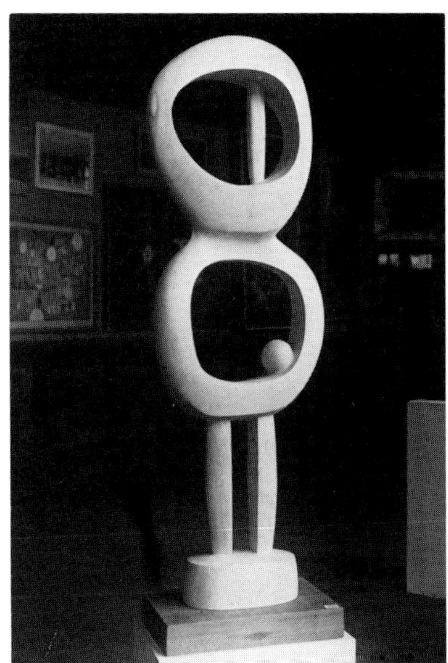

16 **Figure** 1937
Sycamore h.46 (114)
Government Art Collection

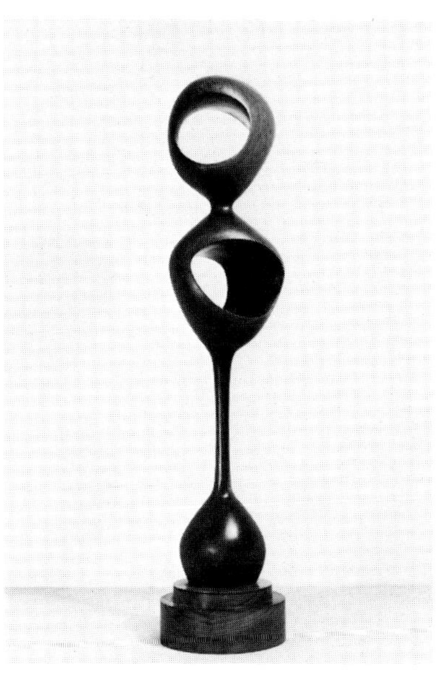

17 **Teak Figure** 1937
Teak h.25 (64)
Bridget John

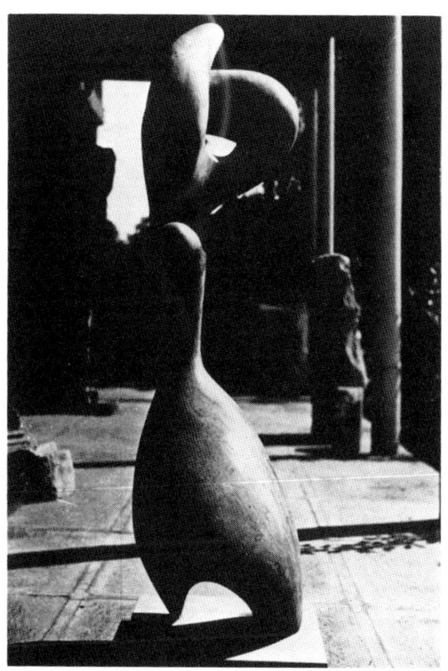

18 **Standing Figure** 1938
Elm h.42½ (108)
Georgian Gallery, Donaghadee

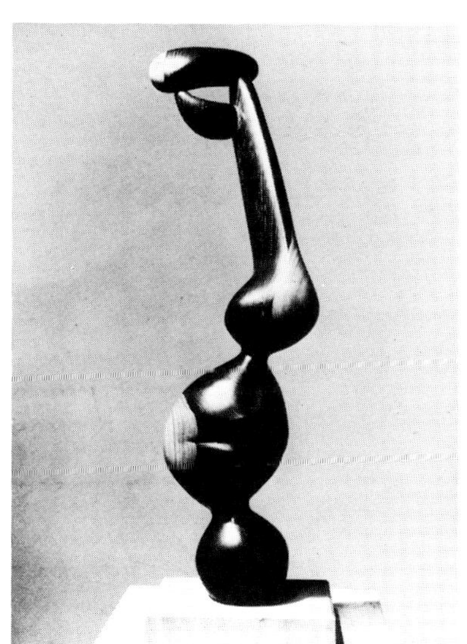

19 **Profile** 1939-40
Lignum vitae h.24 (60)
Tate Gallery

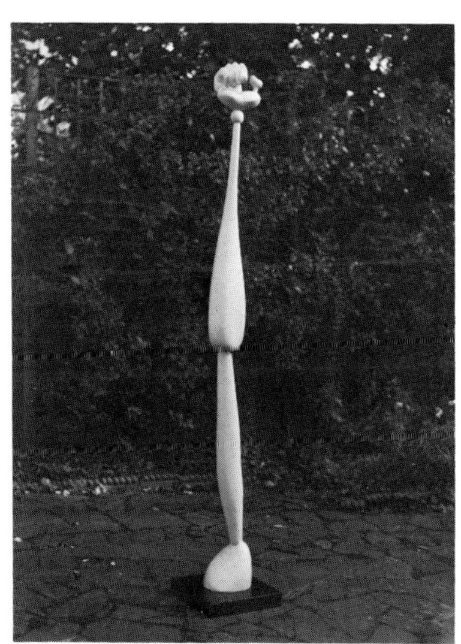

20 **The Long Arm** 1939
(reworked 1945)
Lime h.73 (185)
The Artist

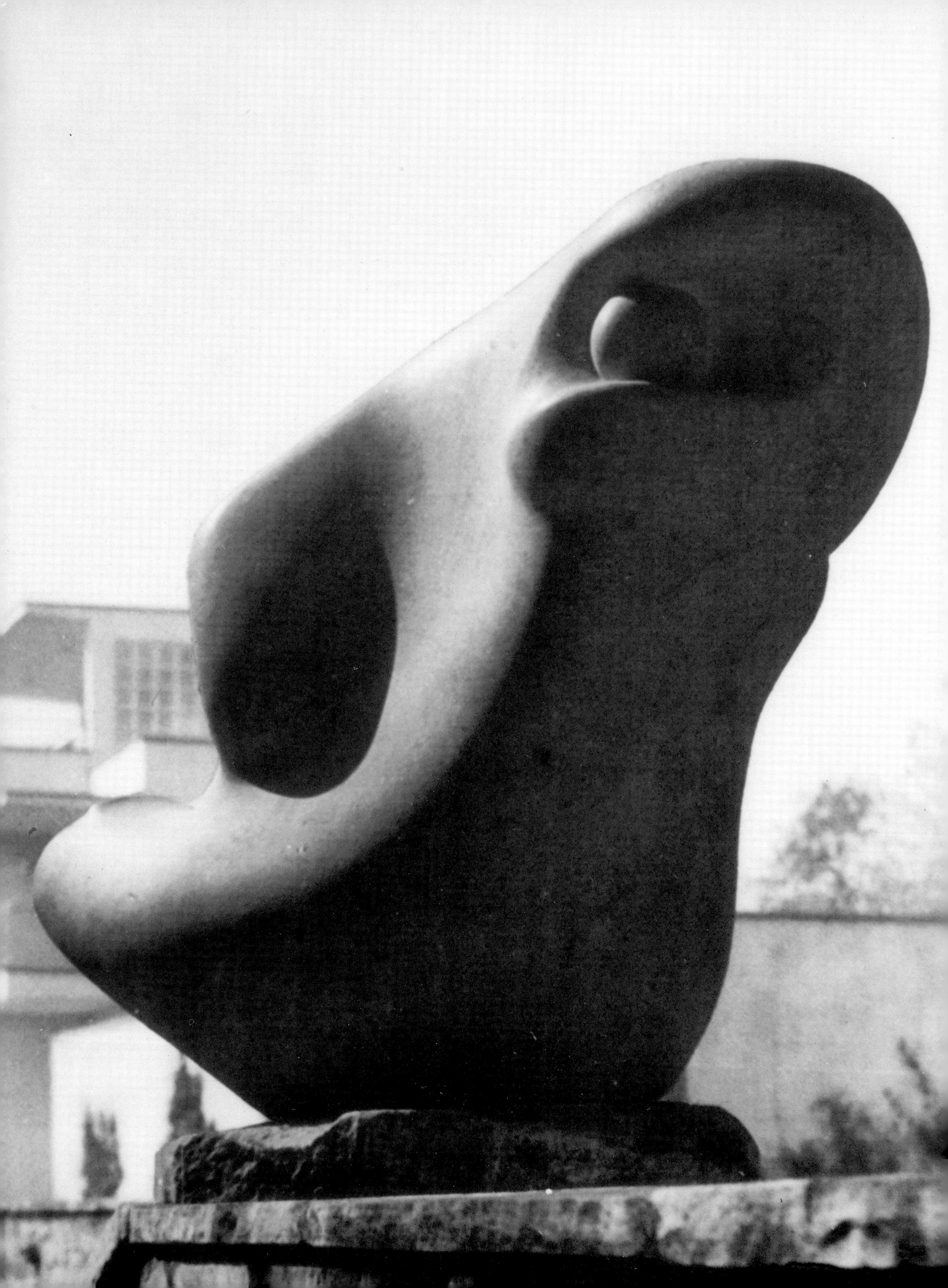

II Stone Carvings 1938-1939

With this group of sculptures, mostly carved from the irregularly hewn shapes that he ordered from Hoptonwood Quarry on the occasion of his visit there with Moore and Gerrard in 1937, McWilliam made a major contribution to European Surrealist sculpture. In most of them (cat.22-26, and 28) he took the idea of the complete fragment, which derived from Rodin, and which had been developed with profound implications by Brancusi and Arp, and with great originality and wit, improvised upon the theme in a totally unexpected way. By fragmenting the head alone, and presenting it as in itself the basis for symbolic biomorphic trans-formations, he introduced an element of sinister portent and dark humour into forms whose primary affect had been more usually felt as comfortingly maternal. In these powerful works, displaced eyes seem suddenly vulnerable, as if the sockets might crush them, or they might roll out of their position; the disembodied head assumes the character of the reclining torso, as if it had taken on a grotesque life of its own; and teeth permanently exposed present an emphatically aggressive saw-edge threat. These pieces were made in the period that saw the violence of the Spanish War, the scandal of non-Intervention and the destruction of the Republic, the appeasement of Hitler, and the approach to European war. Like many artists of his generation, McWilliam viewed these events with concern and foreboding. The sculpture he made during those fateful years, utilising the dislocating techniques of surrealism as a means of access to the unconscious, can be seen in retrospect to have a prophetic force.

'Woman with Arms Crossed' (cat.27) and 'Mother and Child' (cat.21) may seem to embody aspects of a more hopeful and comforting vision, but the oddly crossed breasts of the woman, and the tenuous balance of the child, are disturbingly at odds with their ostensible subjects.

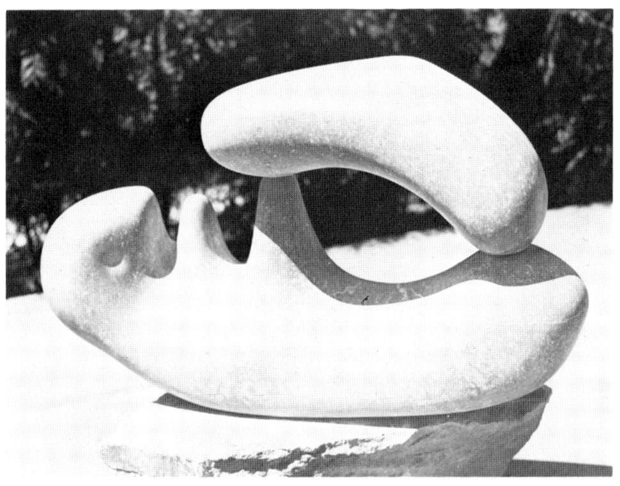

21 Mother and Child 1938
Roman stone l.23 (60)
Private Collection

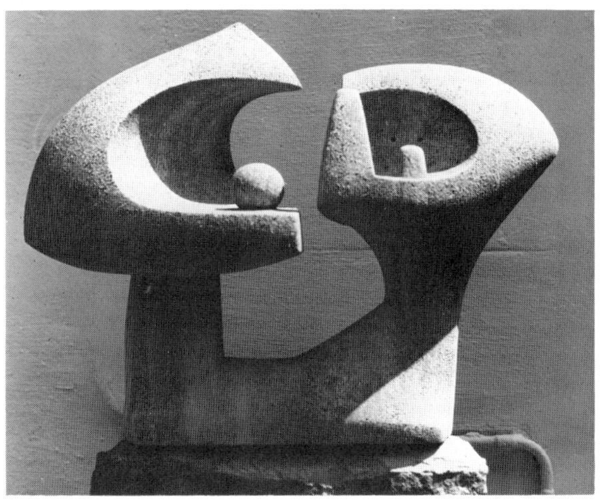

22 Two Forms 1938
Hoptonwood stone l.27 (68)
Bridget John

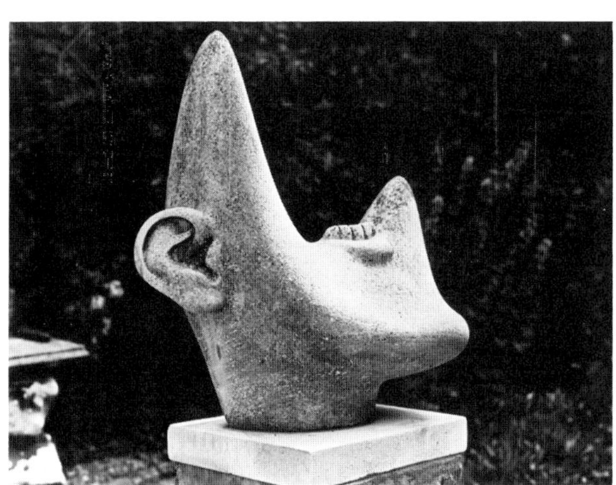

23 Mandible 1938
Hoptonwood stone l.23½ (60)
Private Collection

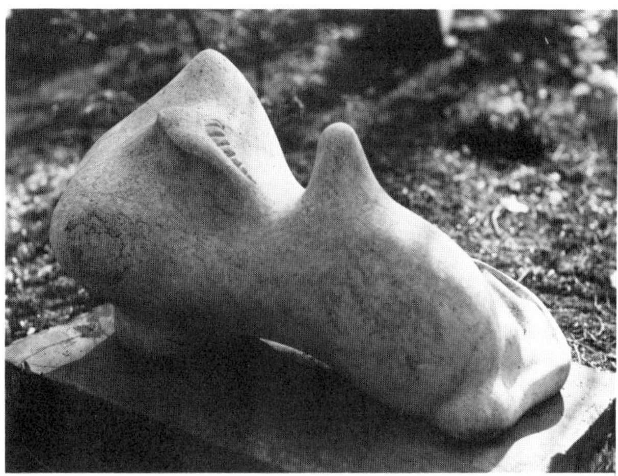

24 Reclining Head 1938
Hoptonwood stone l.30 (76)
The Artist

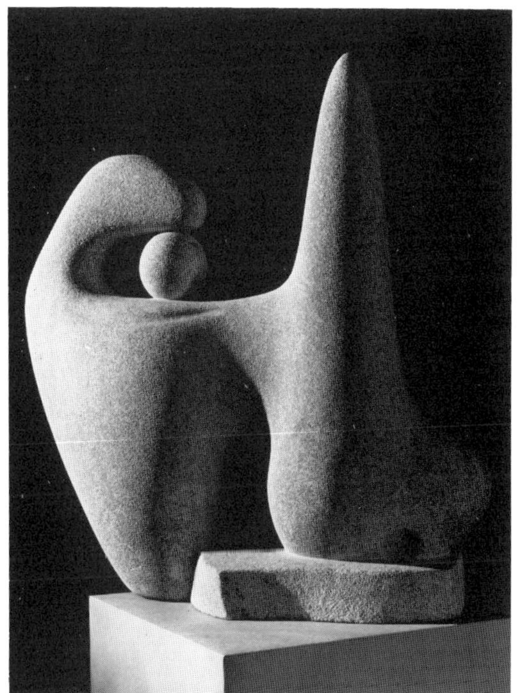

25 Eye, Nose and Cheek 1939
Hoptonwood stone h.35 (90)
Tate Gallery

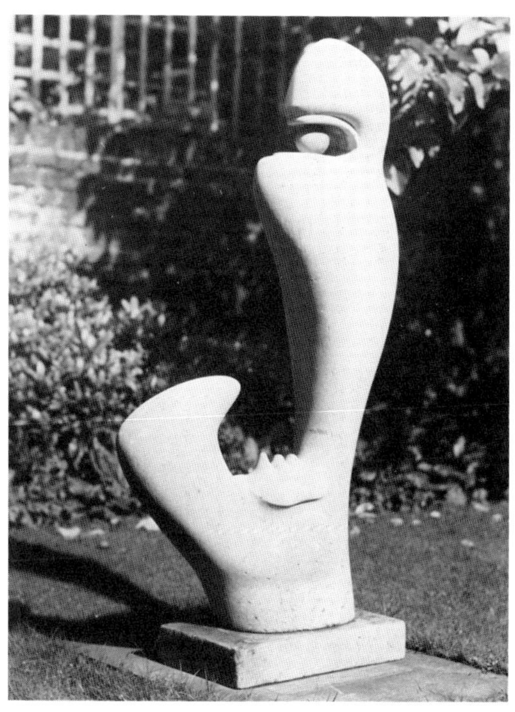

26 Spanish Head 1939
Hoptonwood stone h.51 (130)
The Artist

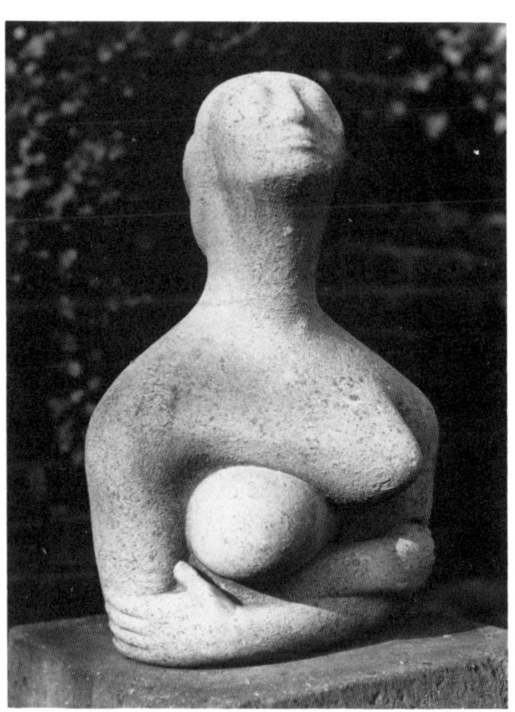

27 Woman with Arms Crossed 1939
Hoptonwood stone h.21½ (54)
George and Maura McClelland

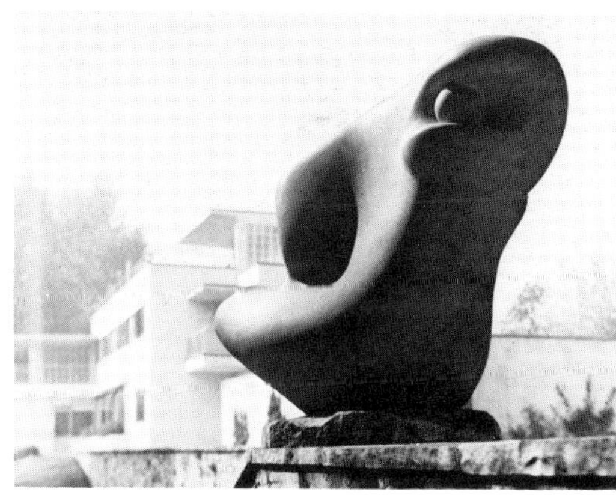

28 Head 1939
Hoptonwood stone l.25½ (65)
The Artist

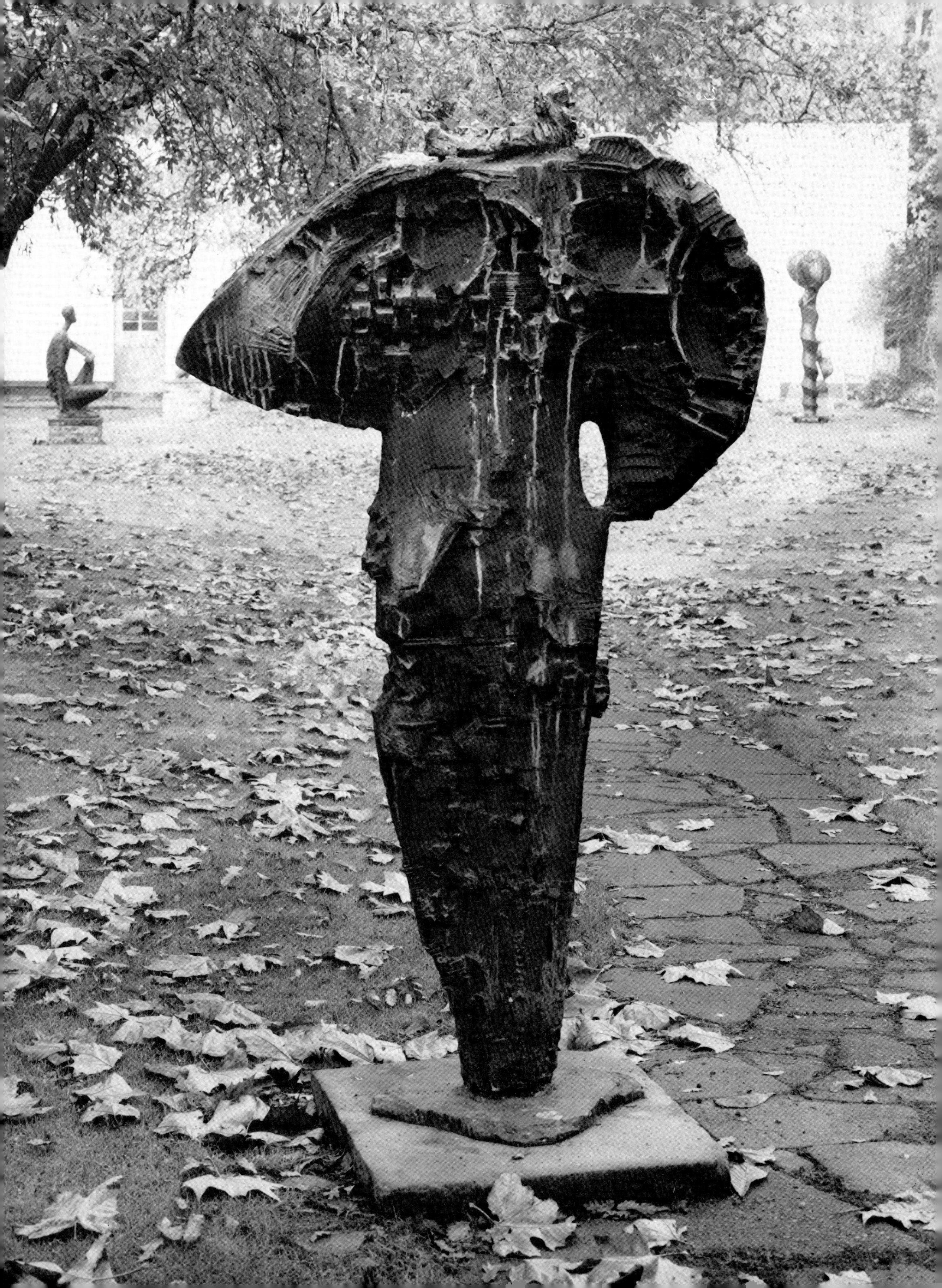

III   Works in Various Media 1946-1960

On his return from India in 1946, McWilliam began to experiment in new media and draw upon a wide range of sources for his imagery. A handful of pieces, represented here by 'The Potter's Wife' (cat.30) and 'Bengali Figure' (cat.29), were modelled in terracotta, and reflected his experience of the temple sculpture he had seen and photographed in Bengal. He worked in cast stone, developing the device of the omitted torso to its extremest form in 'Kneeling Man' (cat.31) where the figure is entirely represented by limbs and head, and complicating the concept by working with two figures and one or part of one torso, as in 'Man and Wife' (cat.34) and 'Father and Daughter' (cat.35). This latter drew more directly than hitherto on conventions of figurative statuary, with hints of the classical, which are more explicitly present in the elmwood 'Roman Matron' (cat.32).

Two major stone carvings made towards the end of the 'forties recapitulated the 'fragmented head' theme of ten years before. There is in these pieces a deadpan directness of reference to classical models that is crucial to their satiric effect. 'Head in Extended Order' (cat.33) may refer indeed to the time-honoured practice in art schools of presenting sculpture students with cast fragments of Michelangelo's 'David' for copying; both that work and 'Irish Head' (cat.36) comment on the device, common to Moore and Hepworth, of the sculpture in two or more parts arranged in an ordered relationship. These works have also a Surrealist antecedence: 'Head in Extended Order' pays conscious homage to Magritte's 'l'Evidence Eternelle' of 1930, in which a female nude has been divided into five sections, each framed and hung vertically in correct order; that painting had been hung next to McWilliam's 'object' in the *Surrealist Objects and Poems* exhibition in 1937.

During the 'fifties McWilliam moved progressively from an attenuated, broken-surfaced figuration, modelled on wire armatures and cast in bronze, influenced perhaps by Giacometti and Richier, and very much in the mode of the period, towards more abstract standing relief forms, somewhat like heraldic and symbolic devices. 'Eve' (cat.37) and 'Patriarch' (cat.38) are among the finest examples of his work in the earlier mode; 'Icon' (cat.40), with its memorable and mysterious presence, and distinctive asymmetrical shape, represents the climax of that period of work. 'Man Erect' (cat.39), from the middle of the decade, if untypical of McWilliam's work at that time, is nonetheless an entirely characteristic invention. Inspired by reports of new discoveries of the remains of *Homo erectus*, its shoulders modelled on the human breast bone, the wit of the piece turns upon a recognition of the central force of sexuality in human evolution.

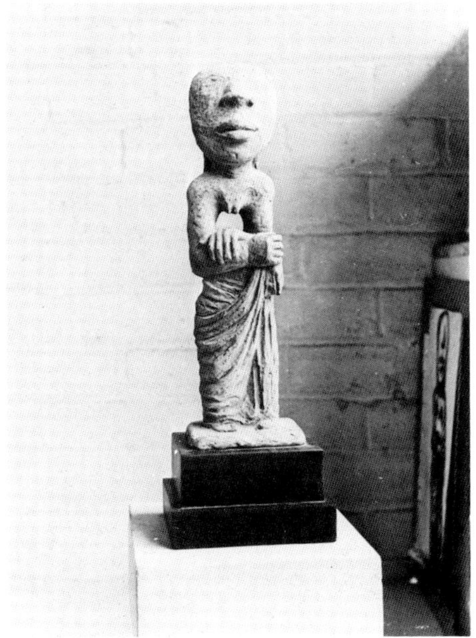

29 **Bengali Figure** 1946
Terracotta h.9 (20)
Mrs Brian Melland

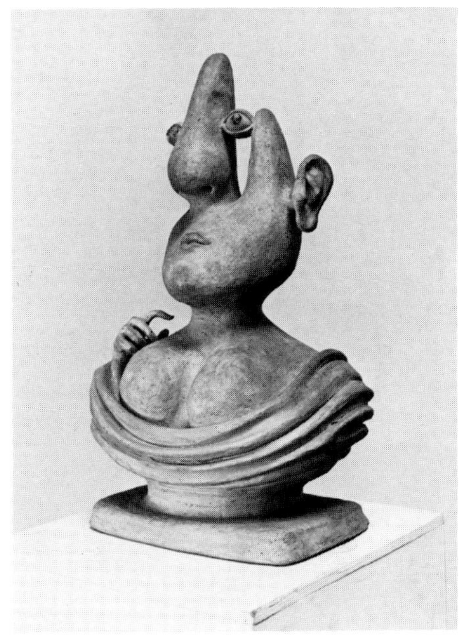

30 **The Potter's Wife** 1947
Bronze h.18½ (45)
Mrs S. Estorick

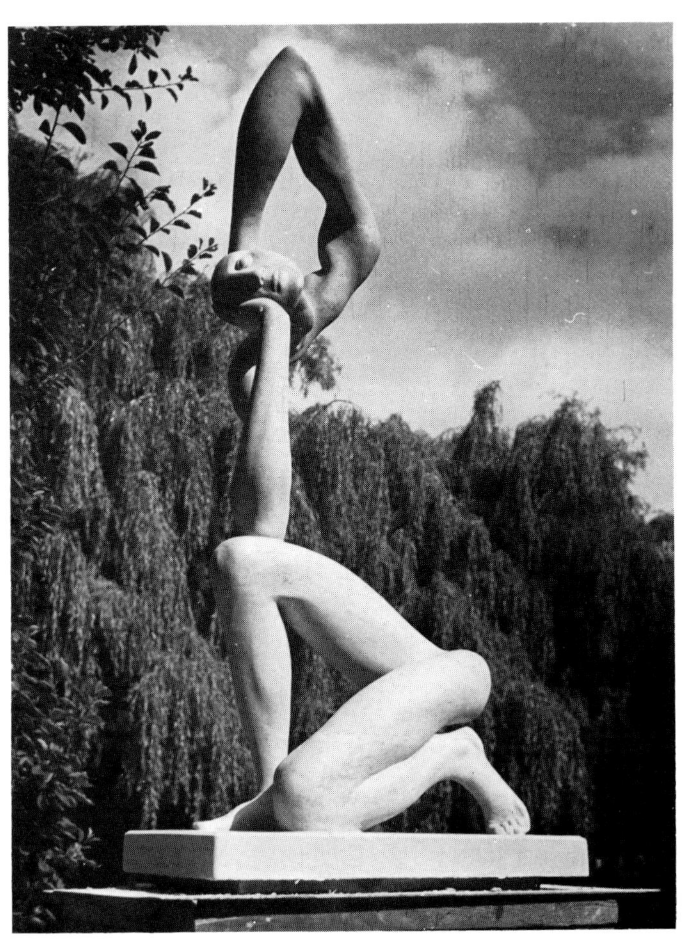

31 **Kneeling Man** 1947
Cast stone h.61 (152)
Sainsbury Centre for Visual Arts,
University of East Anglia

32 Roman Matron 1948
Elm h.41 (104)
Whitford & Hughes, London

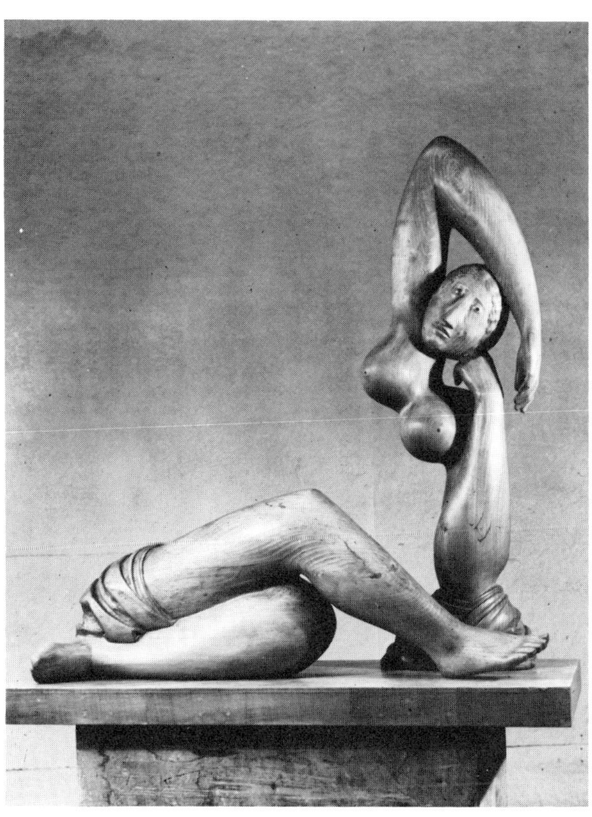

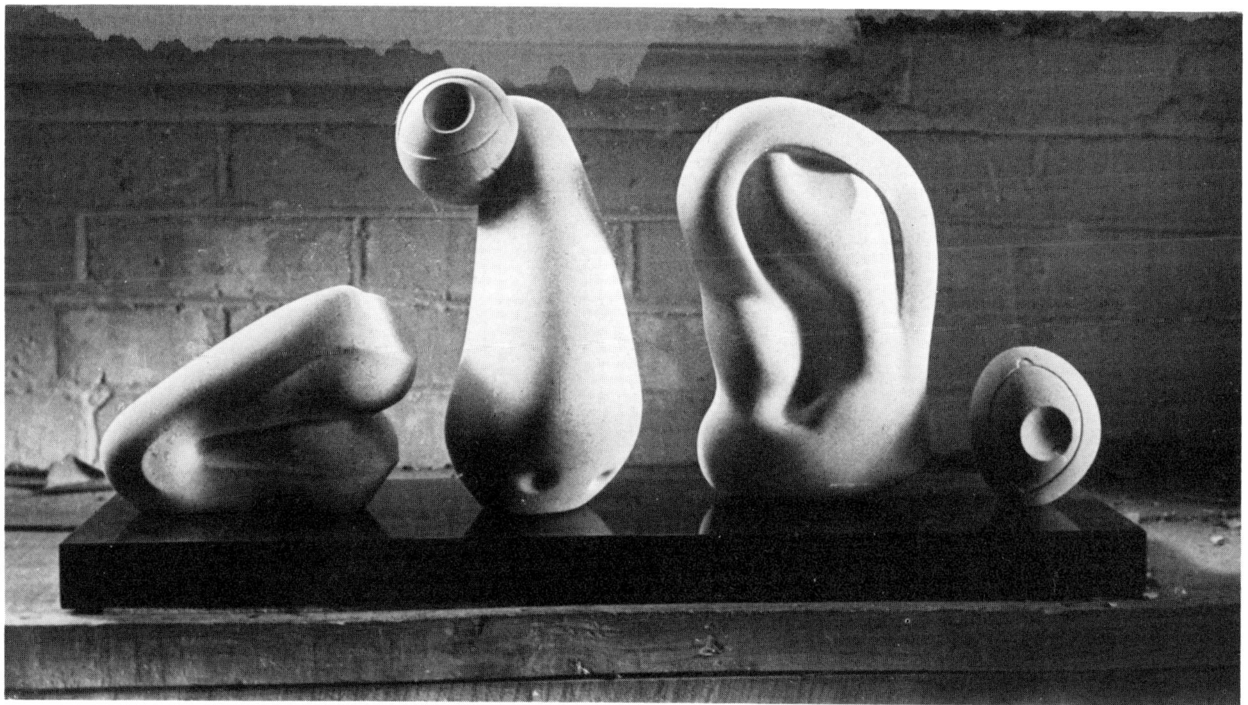

33 Head in Extended Order 1948
Hoptonwood stone l.24 (60)
Private Collection

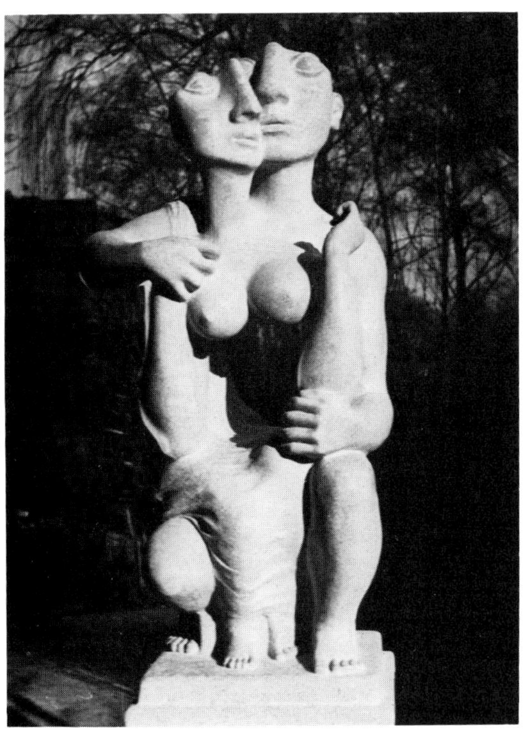

34 Man and Wife 1948
Cast stone h.45 (112)
Ulster Museum, Belfast

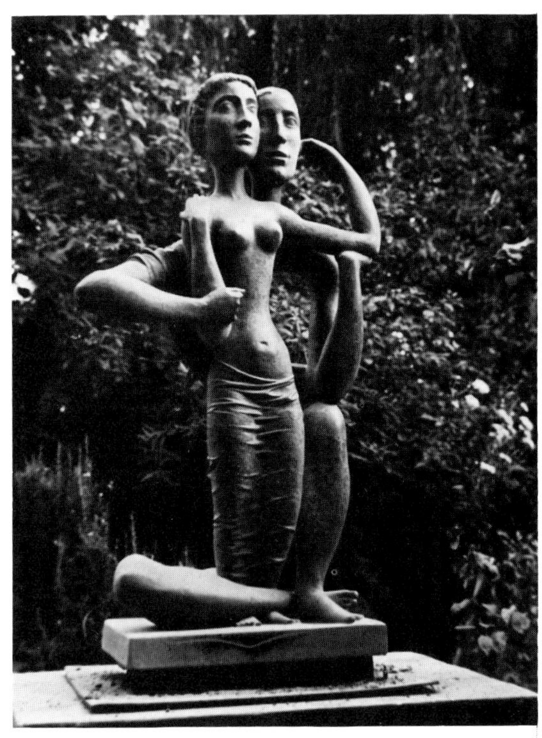

35 Father and Daughter 1949
Cast stone h.43 (108)
*Robert and Lisa Sainsbury Collection, Sainsbury
Centre for Visual Arts, University of East Anglia*

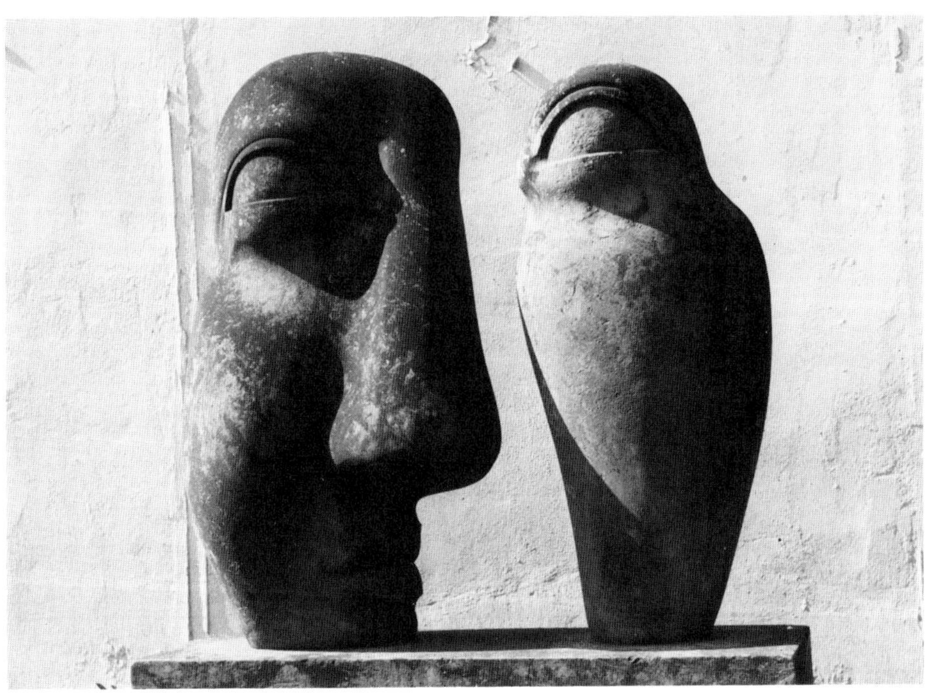

36 Irish Head 1949
Hornton stone h.43 (108)
Allied Irish Bank Collection

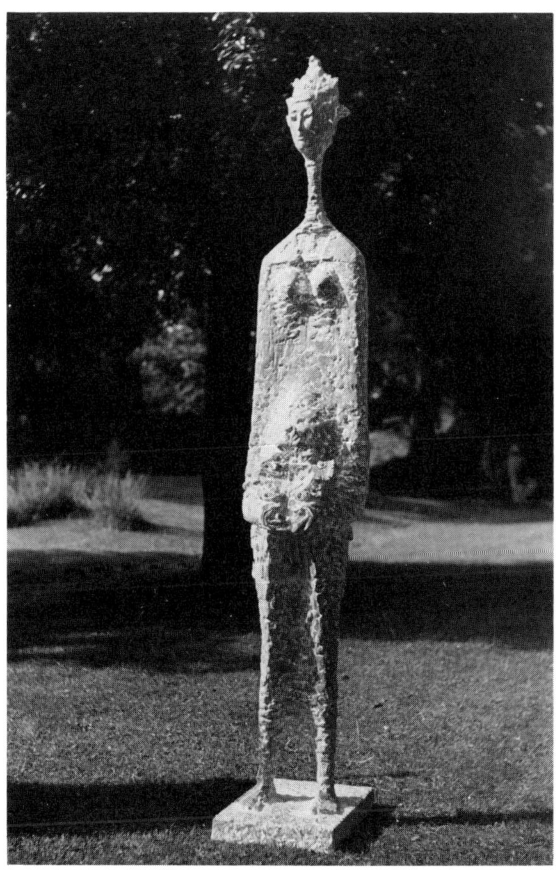

37 **Eve** 1953
Bronze h.75 (190)
Private Collection

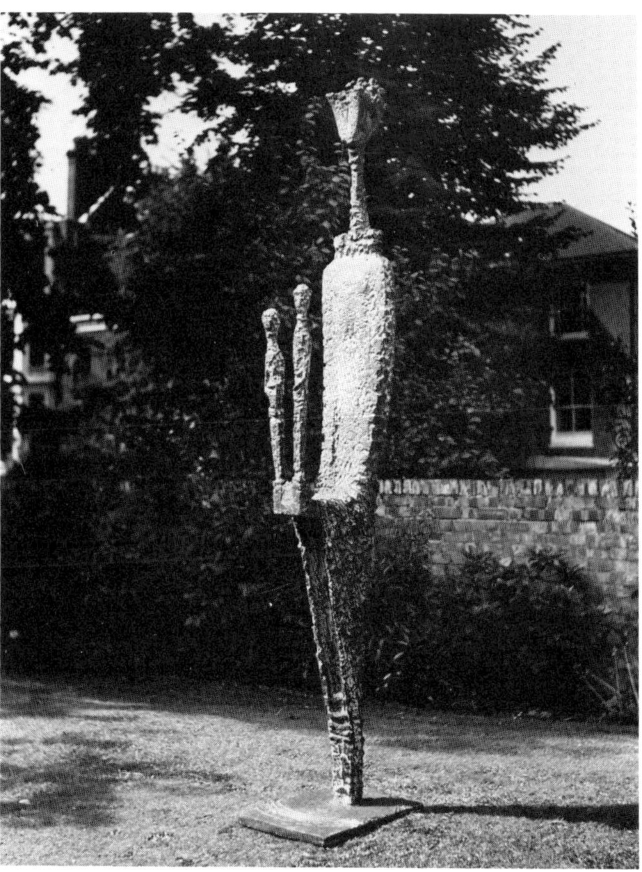

38 **Patriarch** 1953
Composite h.96 (244)
George and Maura McClelland

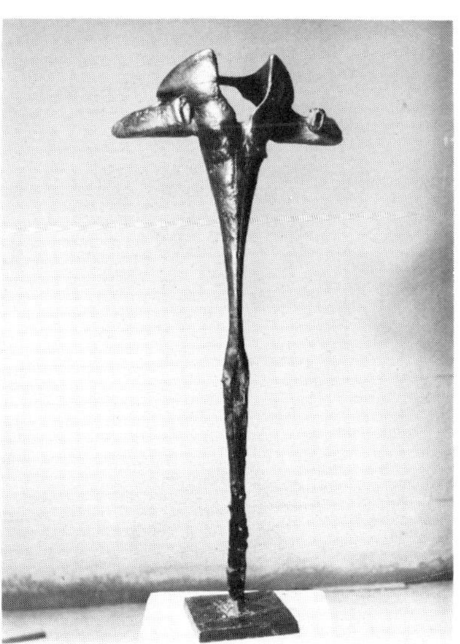

39 **Man Erect** 1955
Bronze h.51 (152)
The Artist

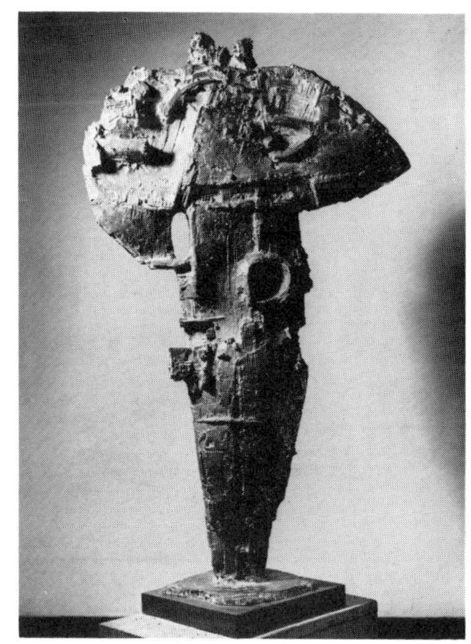

40 **Icon** 1960
Bronze h.63 (160)
The Artist

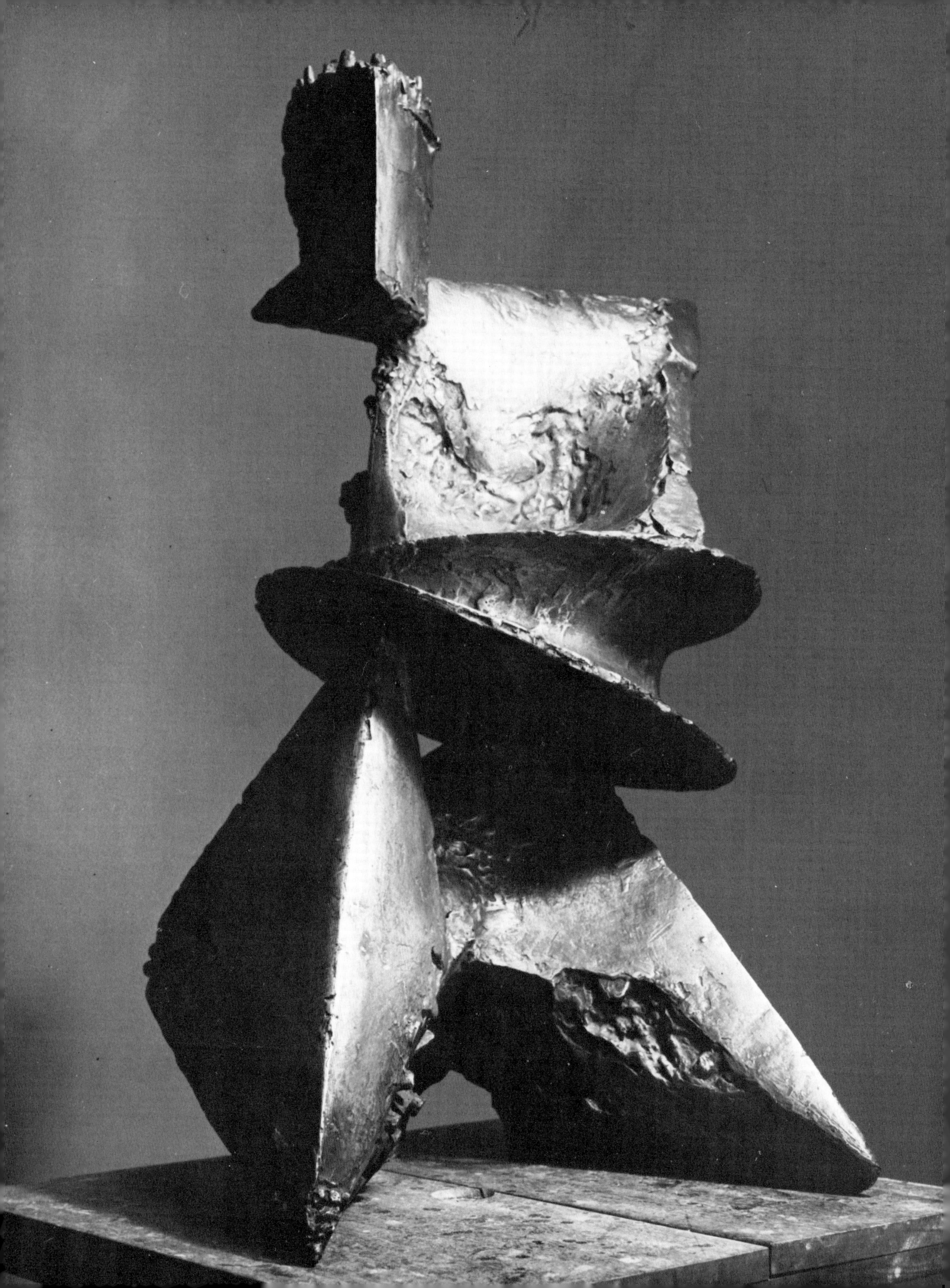

IV Bronze Figures 1962-1964

The series of mechanomorphic bronze figures that McWilliam made in the early
'sixties has a remarkable formal unity. As so often in McWilliam's work, one is
aware of an ironic commentary upon the work of Moore. Where Moore's
predominantly horizontal figures recline, their weighty mass earth-bound and
imitative of the landscape, the rolling hills and caverns of mother earth herself,
McWilliam's figures are active, waking up, turning over, sitting up. Their forms,
derived from the engine and its turning shafts, and from the tripartite mechanical
articulations of insect morphology, are even so immediately recognisable as
humanly dynamic. They propose activity, kinesis, as the predominant human
characteristic: against a static monumentality they assert the sculptural possibilities
of a vital representation of movement. And they indicate the mechanical as a
metaphorically potent model for the human form in motion. In doing so these
works take up again issues to do with movement in space that go back in different
ways to Rodin and to Boccioni and the futurists, without being in any way imitative
of those earlier figures.

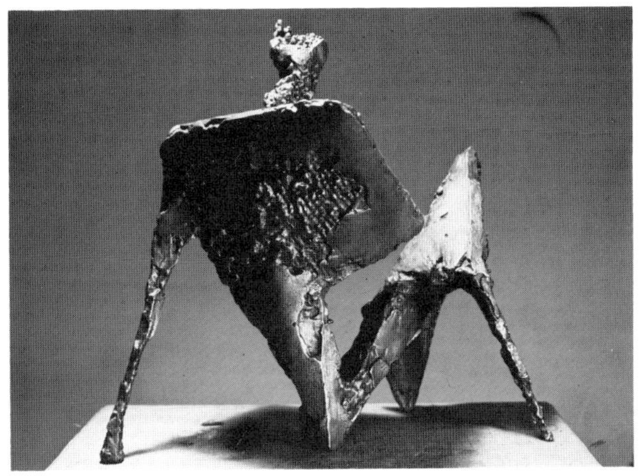

41 **Sitting Up Figure** 1962
Bronze l.22 (56)
Private Collection

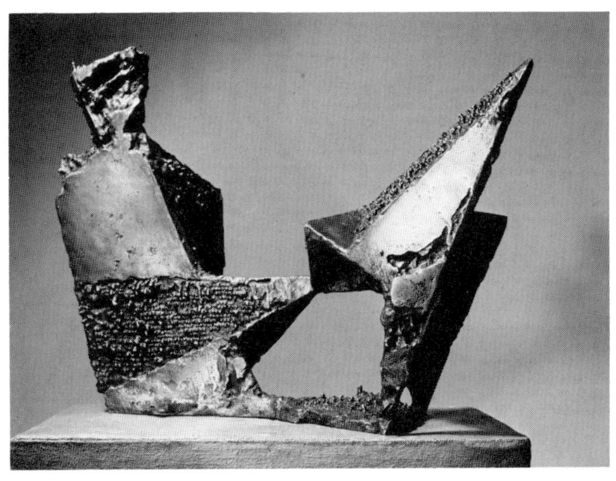

42 **Angular Figure** 1962
Bronze l.34 (87)
Peter and Caroline Barker-Mill

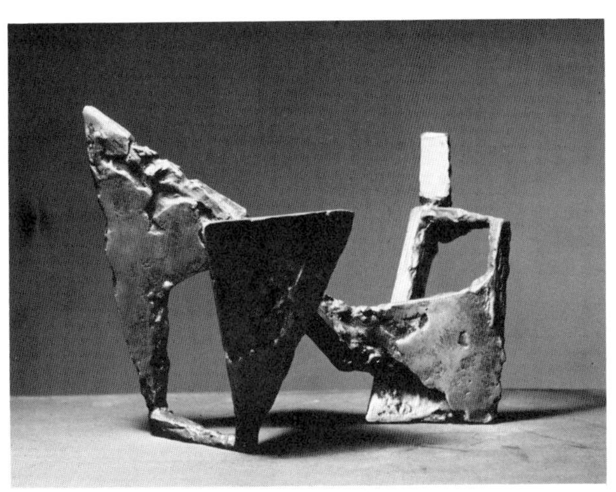

43 **Open Figure** 1962
Bronze l.14 (35)
Miss Maria McAllister

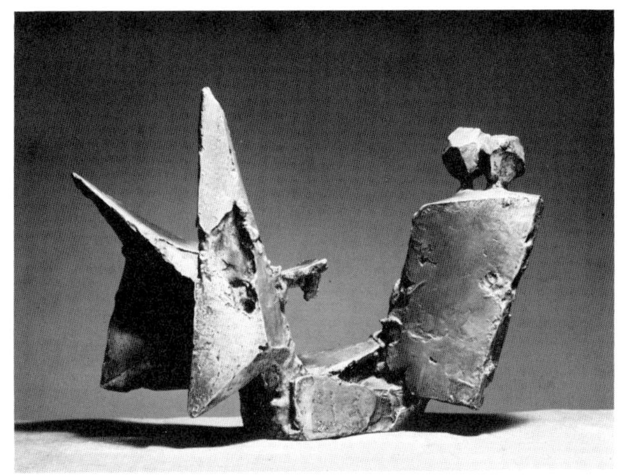

44 **Two Headed Figure** 1962
Bronze l.22 (56)
The Artist

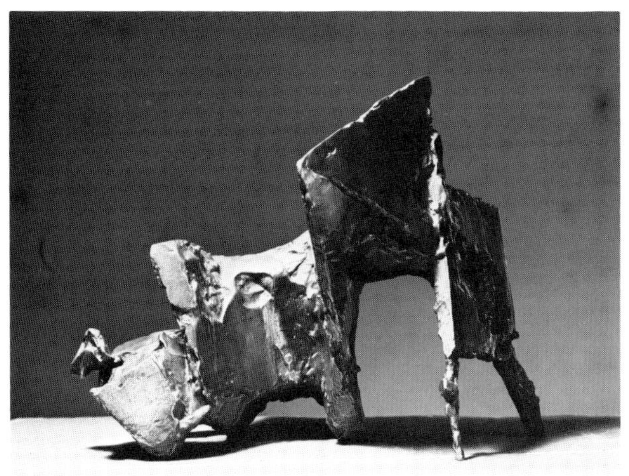

45 **Turning-over Figure** 1962
Bronze l.18 (46)
The Artist

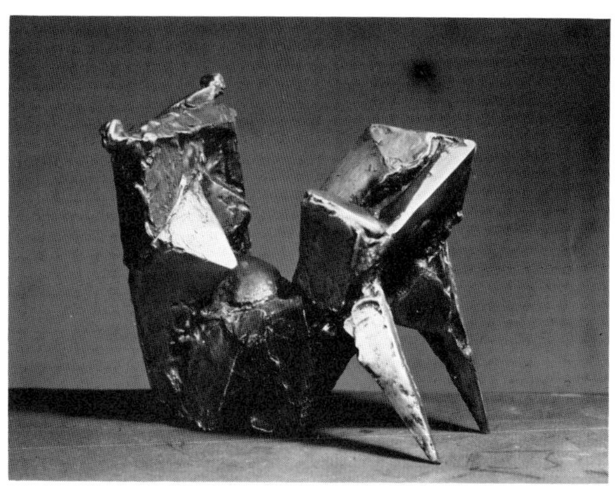

46 **Waking Up Figure** 1962
Bronze l.10 (25.5)
Don Jordan

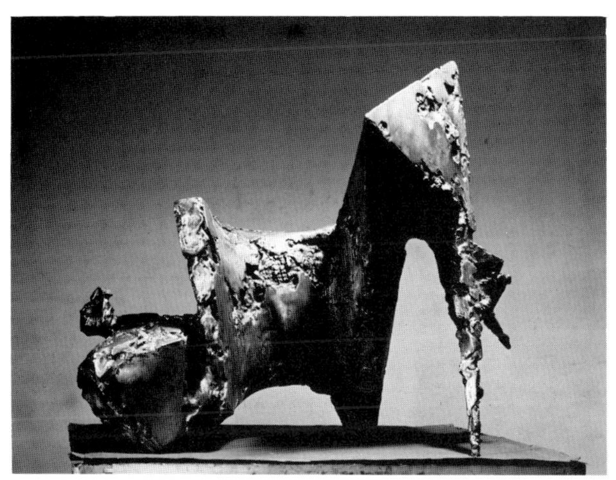

47 **Rolling Over Figure** 1963
Bronze l.30 (76)
The Artist

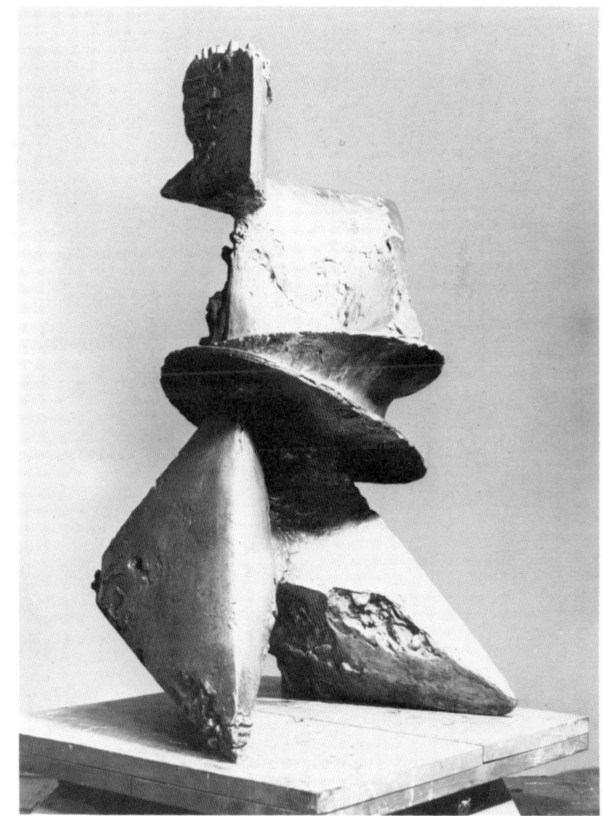

48 **Figure with Hoops** 1964
Bronze h.35½ (90)
The Artist

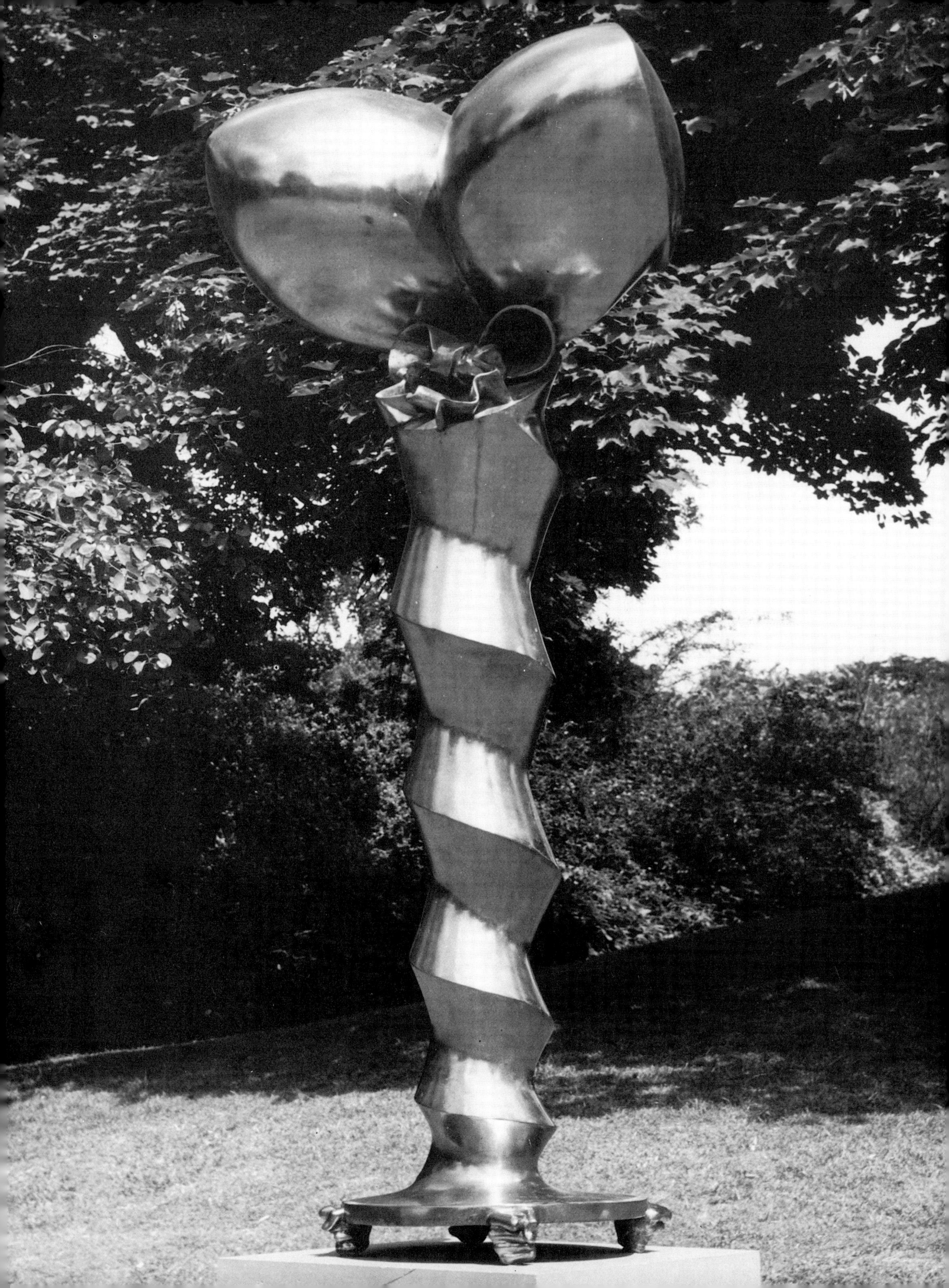

V Bronze 'Bean' Sculptures 1965-1966

The Bean bronzes, inspired by a *coco de mer* (the huge two-lobed nut of the Seychelles palm) that McWilliam had in his studio for some time before using it as the basis for this series, are the only symmetrical sculptures that McWilliam has made. This has to do with the obvious and richly suggestive congruity of the 'bean', with its central declivity, to double-sided and spherical human physical attributes, to the head, to breasts and buttocks, to vulva and womb. The series represents McWilliam at his most fanciful and capricious, taking the splendidly organic and natural *motif* and subjecting it to cultural and national variations with virtuosic wit. The essential themes are of the dynamics between nature and culture, between sexuality and fecundity and social order and control, between private experience and public image, between feminine and masculine. Underlying the whole performance is an anarchic delight in the abundant fertility of nature and the irrepressible exuberance of sexuality. The keynote work in this respect is the 'May Day Figure' (cat.49), with its spiralling stem (a sort of maypole dance in itself) and its rich ambiguities of reference.

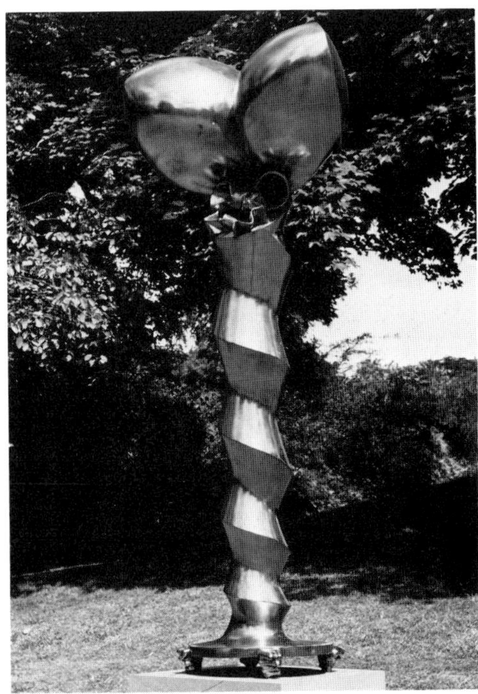

49 May Day Figure 1965
Bronze h.85 (216)
The Artist

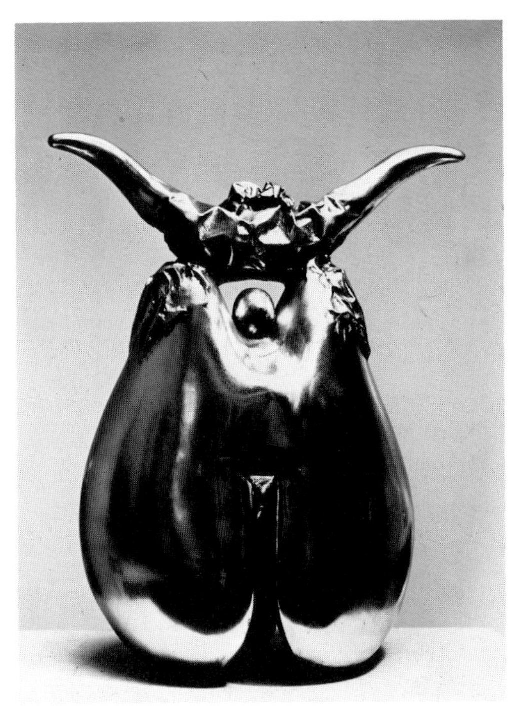

50 Nordic Bean 1965
Bronze h.25 ½ (65)
The Artist

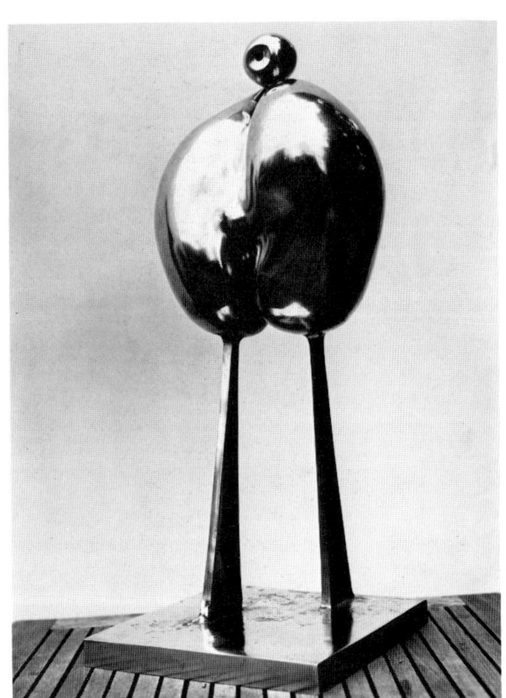

51 Anthropomorphic Bean 1965
Bronze h.31 (79)
The Artist

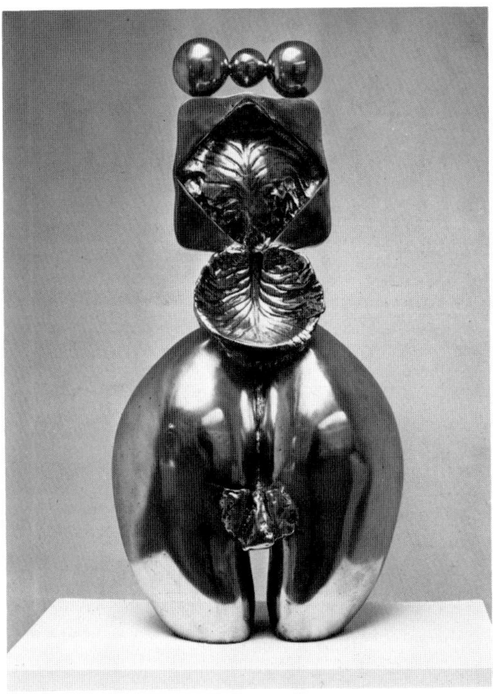

52 Bean with Sauerkraut and Fig Leaf 1965
Bronze h.32 (81)
The Artist

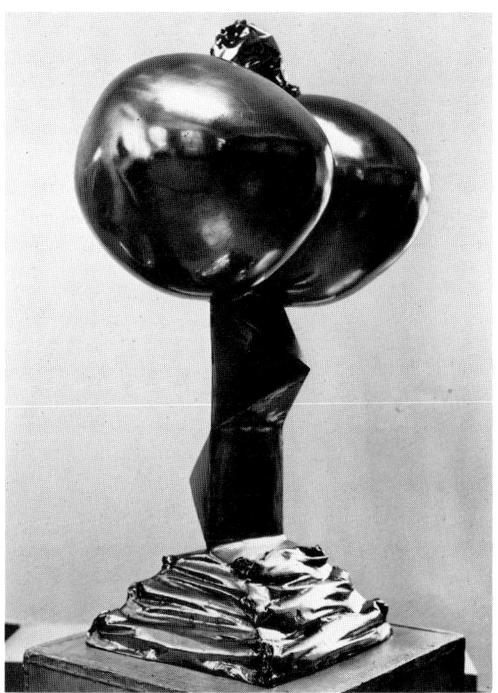

53 **Duplex Bean** 1965
Bronze h.37 (94)
The Artist

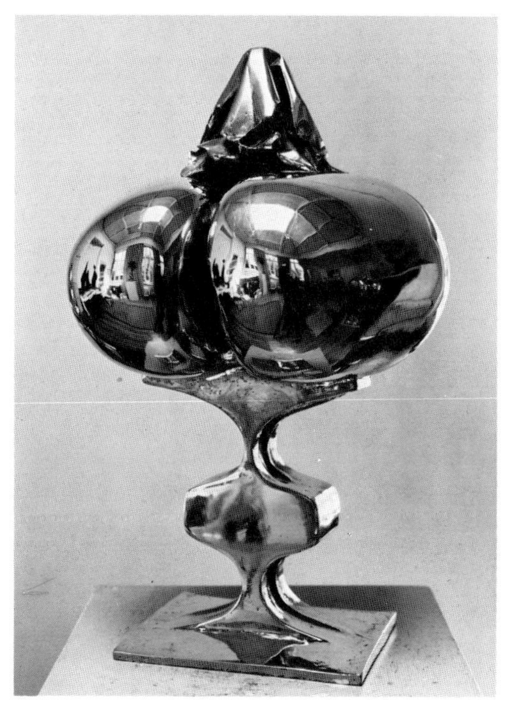

54 **Spanish Bean** 1965
Bronze h.19 (48)
The Artist

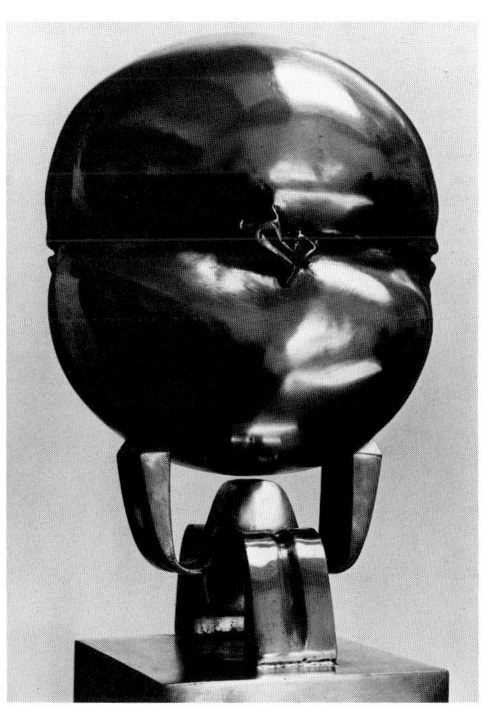

55 **Roman Bean** 1965
Bronze h.22 (56)
The Artist

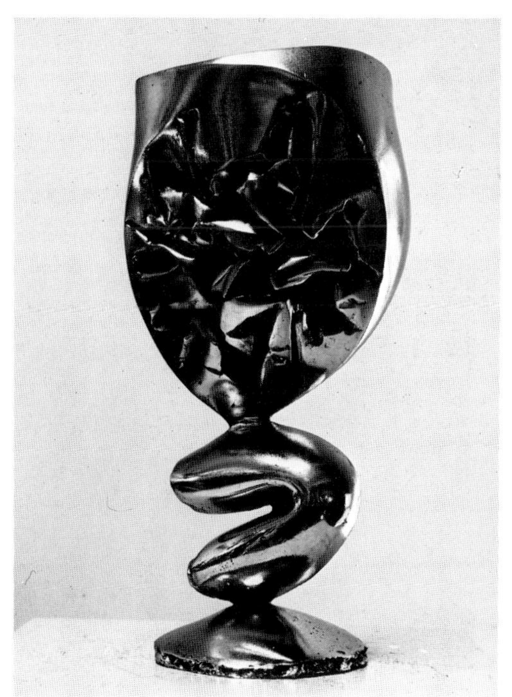

56 **Loving Cup** 1966
Bronze h.14 (35.5)
Private Collection

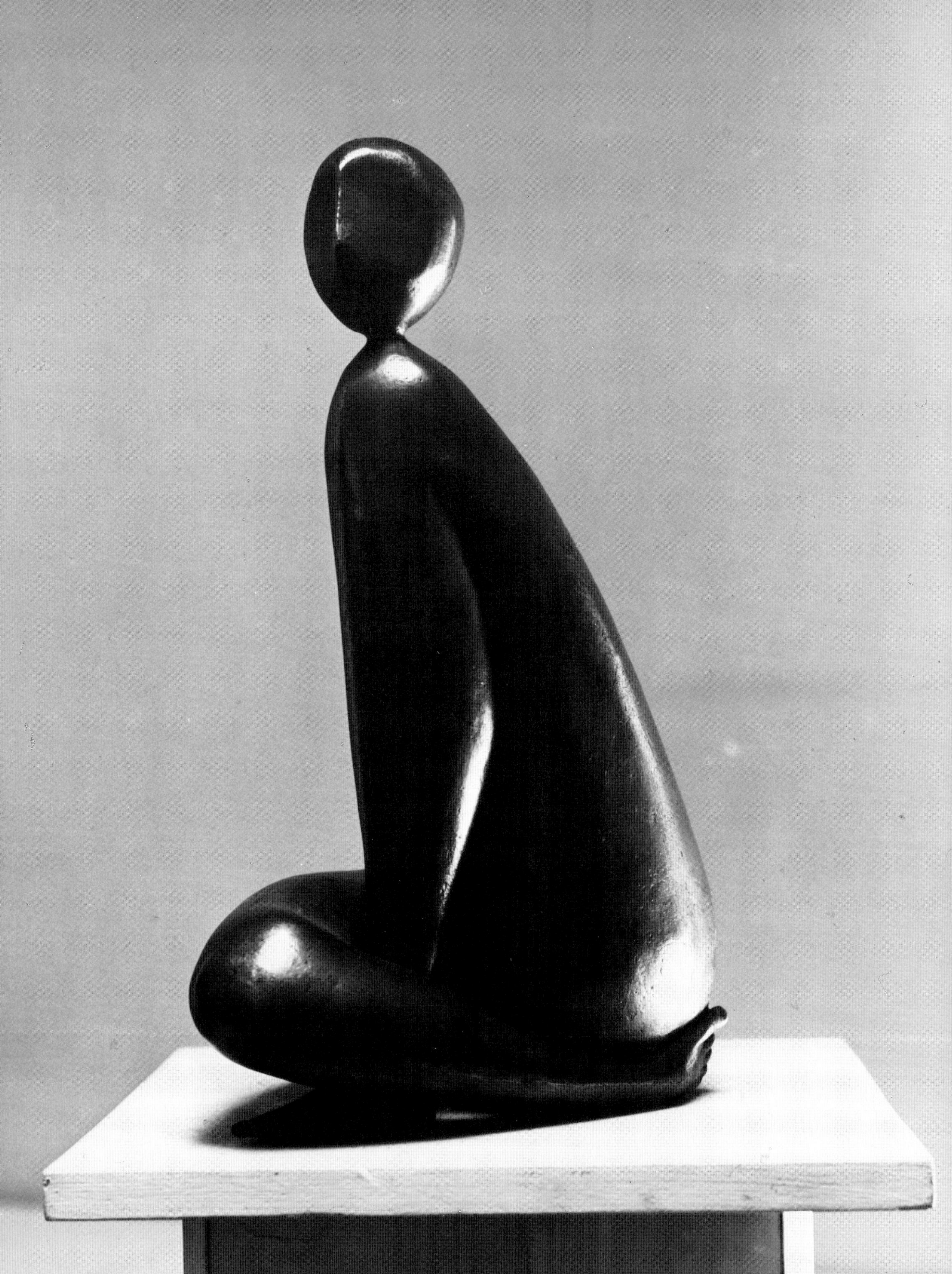

VI   The Bronze 'Legs' 1977-1987

McWilliam turned to the theme of legs after a period of more or less representational sculpture in the early 'seventies, when he had worked on the 'Women of Belfast' and 'Banners' series, both of which had elements of direct political reference. The 'Legs' sculptures mark a return to a more playful and paradoxical imagery, and take both the idea of the complete fragment, and of the eliminated torso, as the basis for a series of unexpected and idiosyncratic improvisations. McWilliam's ability to suggest character and movement with the most economic of means is fully demonstrated in this series, as is his persistent exploitation of the visual joke and the visual pun. The smaller of these works have an elegance and a charm, the qualities of inspired *jeux d'esprit*; the large pieces, notably 'Umbilicus' (cat.60) and 'Legs Static' (cat.61), have a mysterious sculptural presence, the former as of an idol, enigmatic and frontal, the latter as of a figure dematerialising like the Cheshire Cat, her hands incongruously persistent, like its smile.

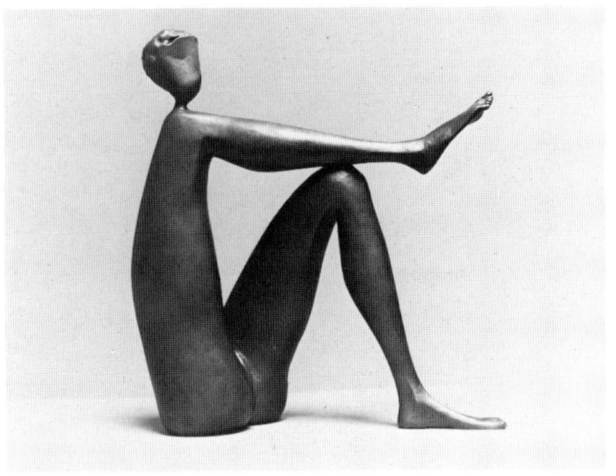

57 **Leg Figure D** 1977
Bronze h.12 (30.5)
The Artist

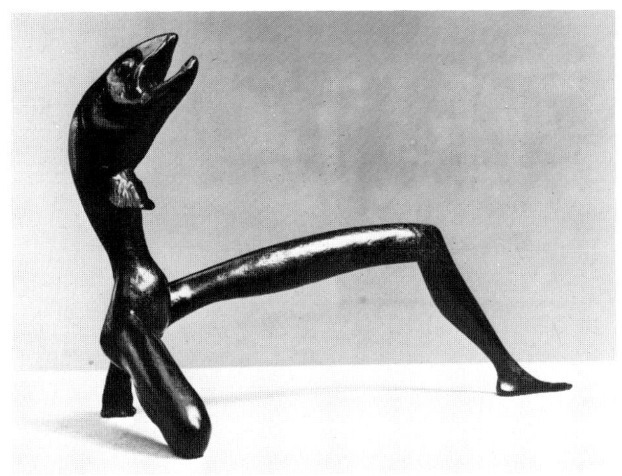

58 **Magritte's Mermaid** 1977
Bronze l.17 (43)
*Shambles Art Gallery, Hillsborough,
Northern Ireland*

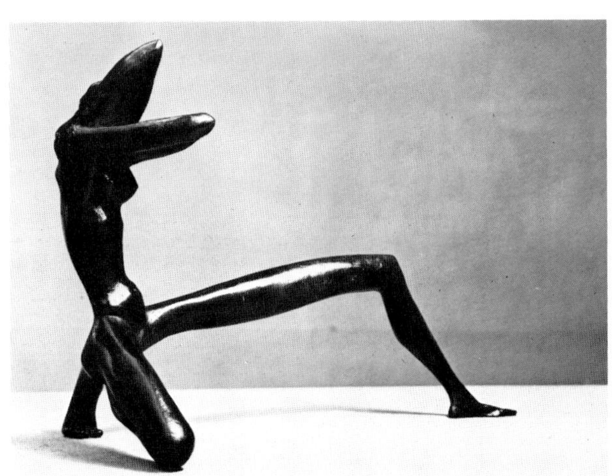

59 **Lady into Fish** 1977
Bronze l.16 (40.5)
The Artist

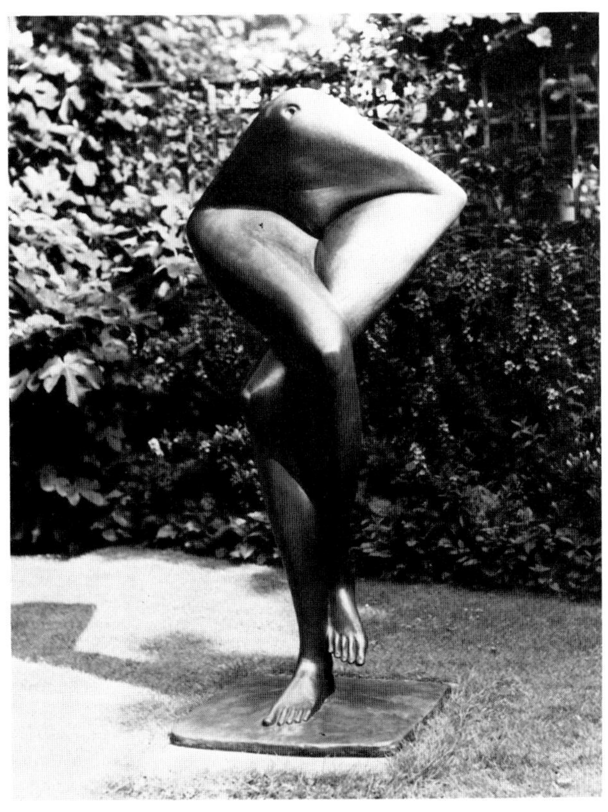

60 **Umbilicus** 1977/8
Bronze h.68 (173)
The Artist

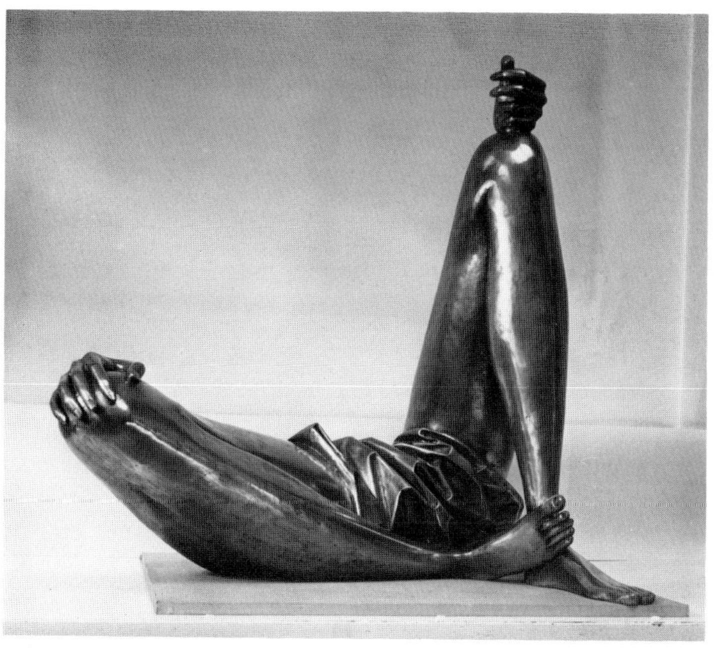

61 Legs Static 1978
Bronze h.39 (99)
The Artist

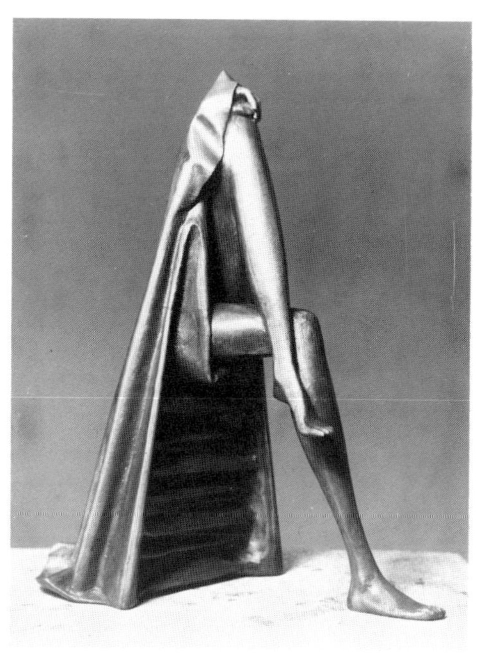

62 Metronome 1978
Bronze h.15 (38)
The Artist

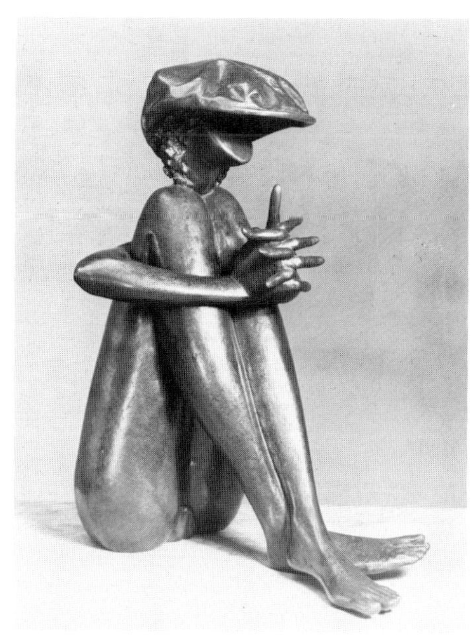

63 Girl with Cloth Cap 1978
Bronze h.18 (46)
The Artist

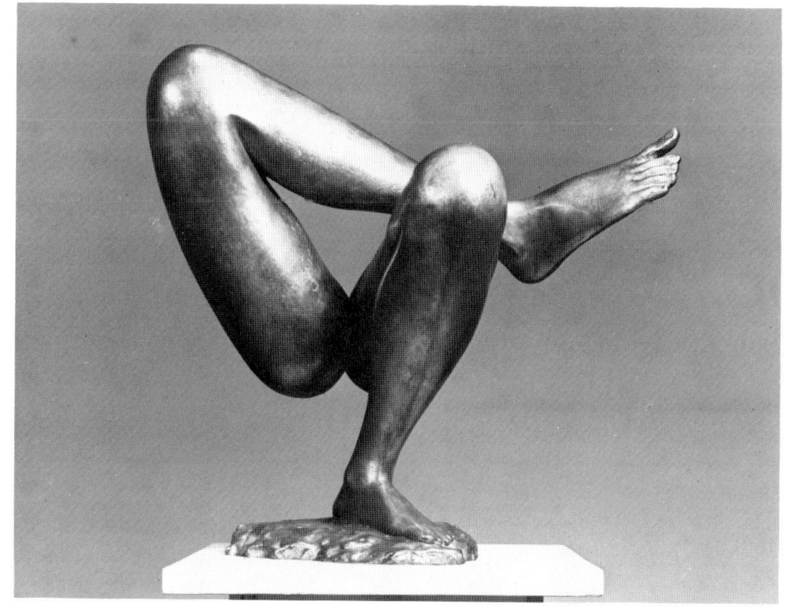

64 Crossed Legs 1978
Bronze h.15 (38)
The Artist

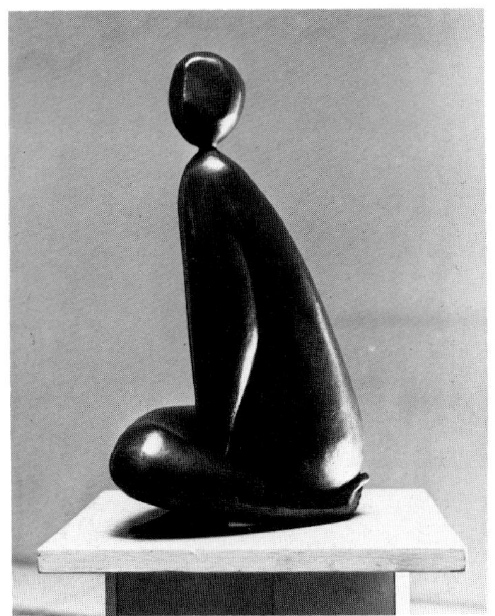

65 Seated Leg Figure 1978
Bronze h.14 (35.5)
David McDonald

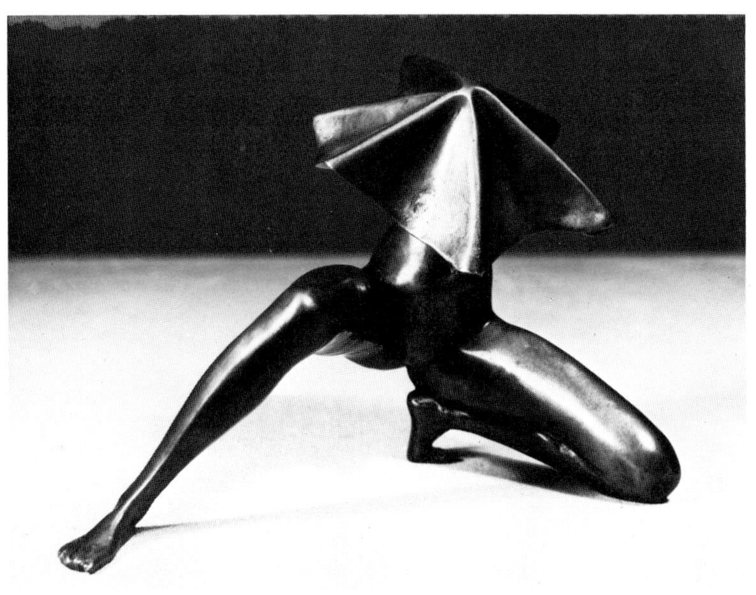

66 Undercover Girl 1978
Bronze l.10 (25.5)
Patrick P. Mackie

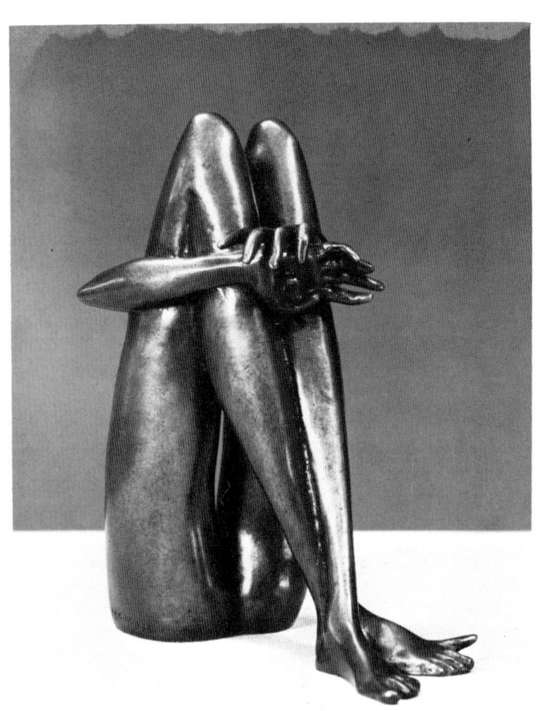

67 Legs Embraced 1978
Bronze h.8½ (22.5)
Private Collection

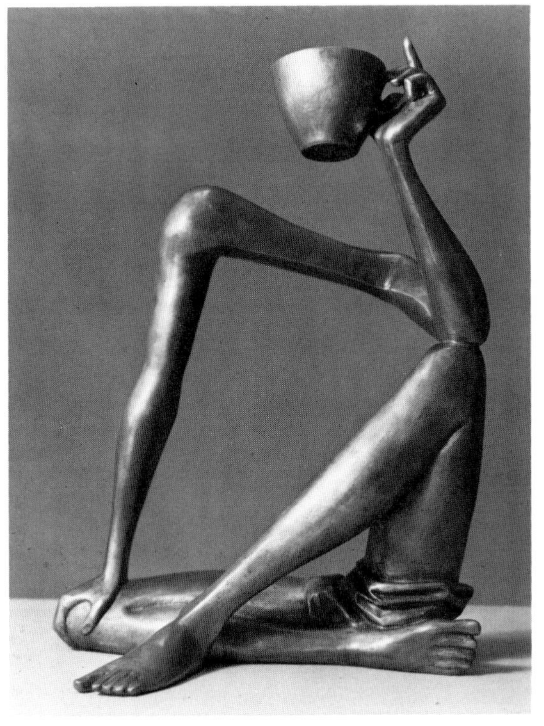

68 Left-Handed Tea Drinker 1981
Bronze h.18½ (47)
The Artist

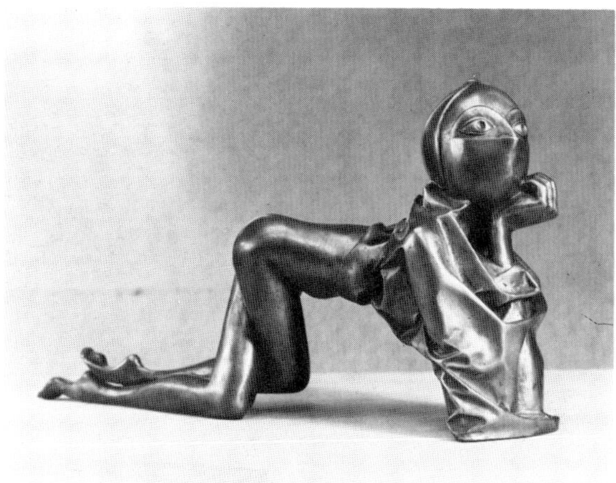

69 **Ms Orissa** 1981
Bronze h. 20 (51)
The Artist

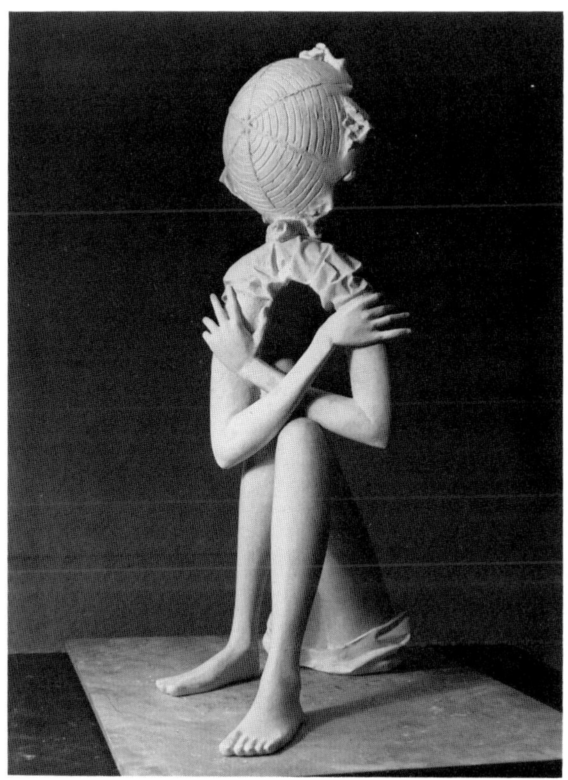

71 **Sun Girl** 1987
Bronze h. 34 (86.5)
The Artist

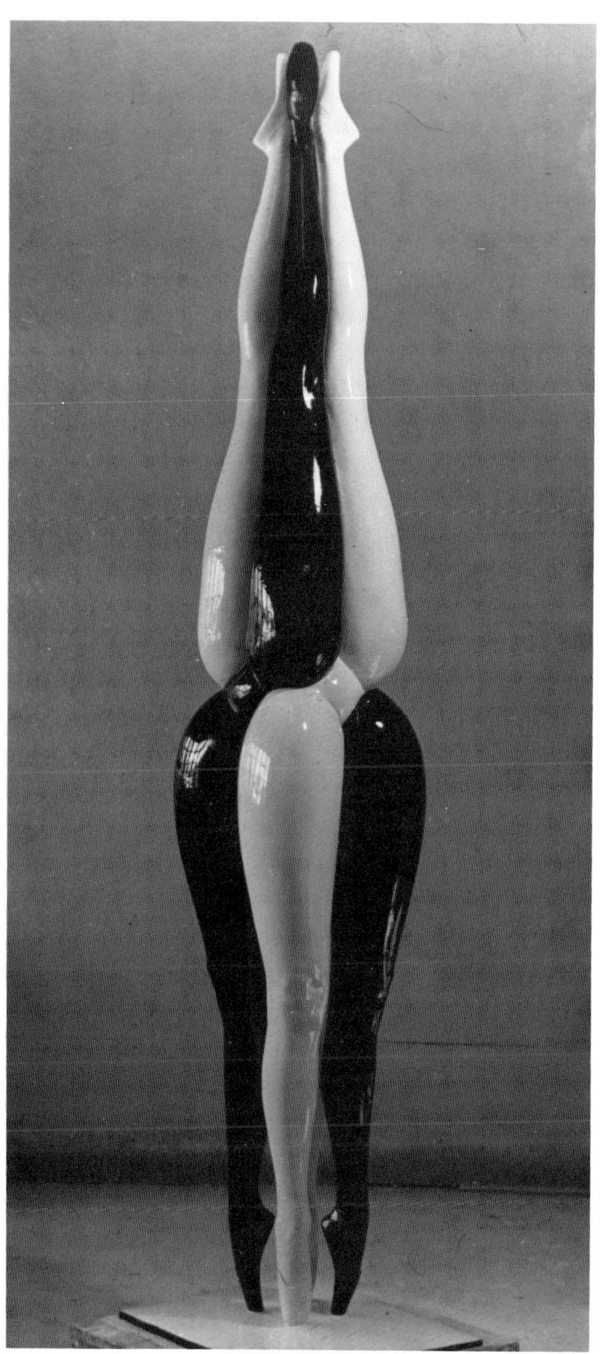

70 **Pas de Quatre** 1981
Painted plaster h. 78 (234)
The Artist

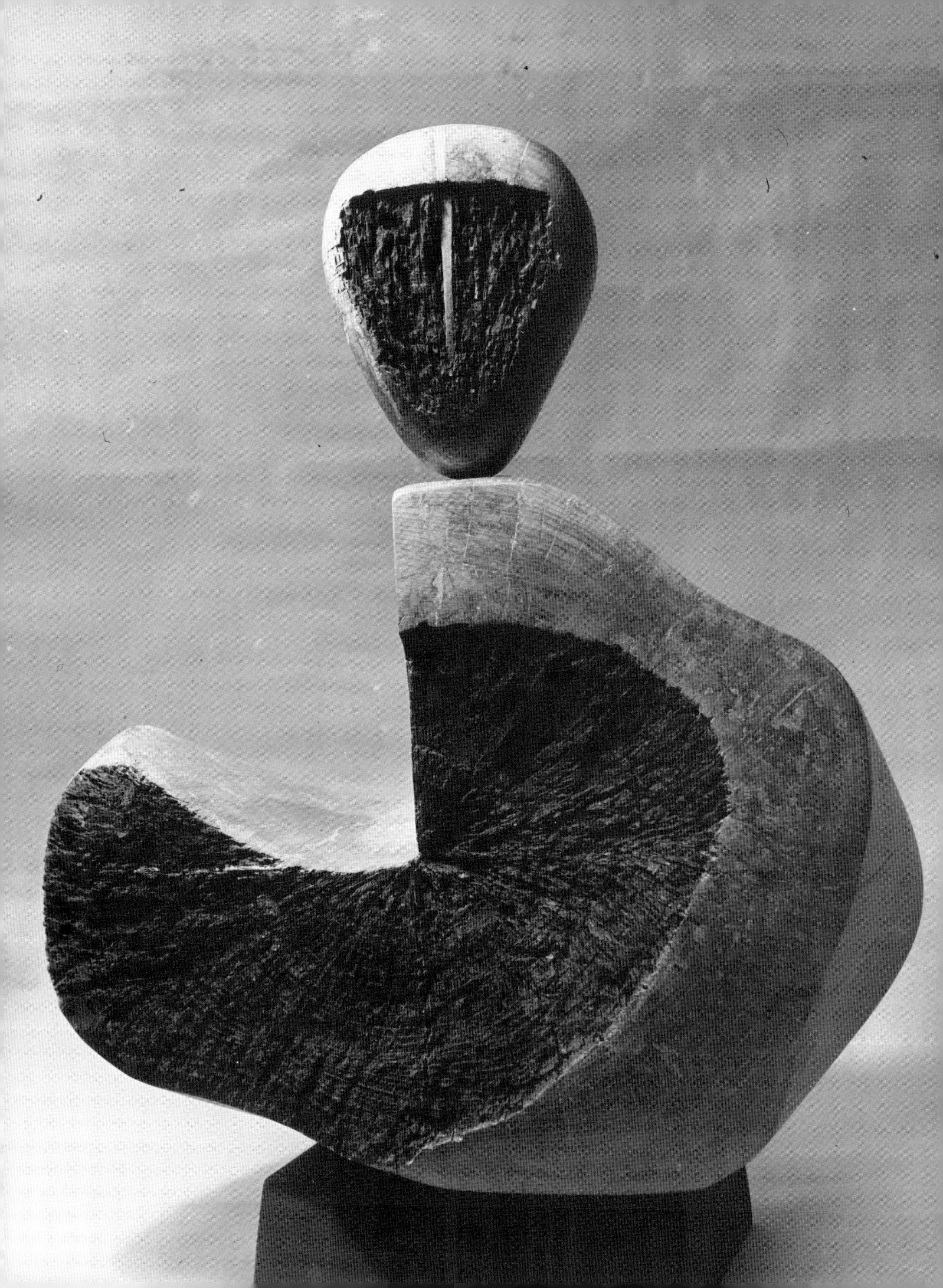

VII Late Carvings 1982-1989

McWilliam's return to carving in the early 'eighties was directly stimulated by two events: the gift from Eugene Rosenberg of some fine pieces of wood; and the rediscovery of certain early works, which he decided could be renovated, and rescued from the oblivion to which they had been consigned since the mid-'thirties. This late flowering of carving has seen McWilliam return to themes and images that have haunted him all his life, in works that have great authority without being in any way solemn. Especially he has come back to the theme of the surreal *personnage*. 'Horizontal Head' (cat.74), 'Egg Head' (cat.75), and 'Poseidon' (cat.77) are examples of this.

The unexpected supply of mulberry wood that the great storm of 1987 made suddenly available had a dynamic effect upon McWilliam, who has always been inspired by what chance may bring. The mysterious group of figures that is the climax of the exhibition is the outcome of a year of intensive work. Their faces and forms are determined as much by the complexly variegated grain and structure of the wood itself (an ironic return to 'truth to materials' perhaps) as by the equally complex and unpredictable imagination of the artist. The cracks, which have continued to proliferate during and after the carving of these pieces, and which are inevitable in unseasoned timber, have been characteristically welcomed by the artist, and incorporated as a linear element in the total design. McWilliam has responded with great sculptural vigour to the fantastic rhythms and turbulences, complications and irregularities of the wood, adding another series of disquietening and ambiguous images to what Bryan Robertson has called his 'poetic repertoire of fantastic biomorphic shapes, anatomies and personages'.

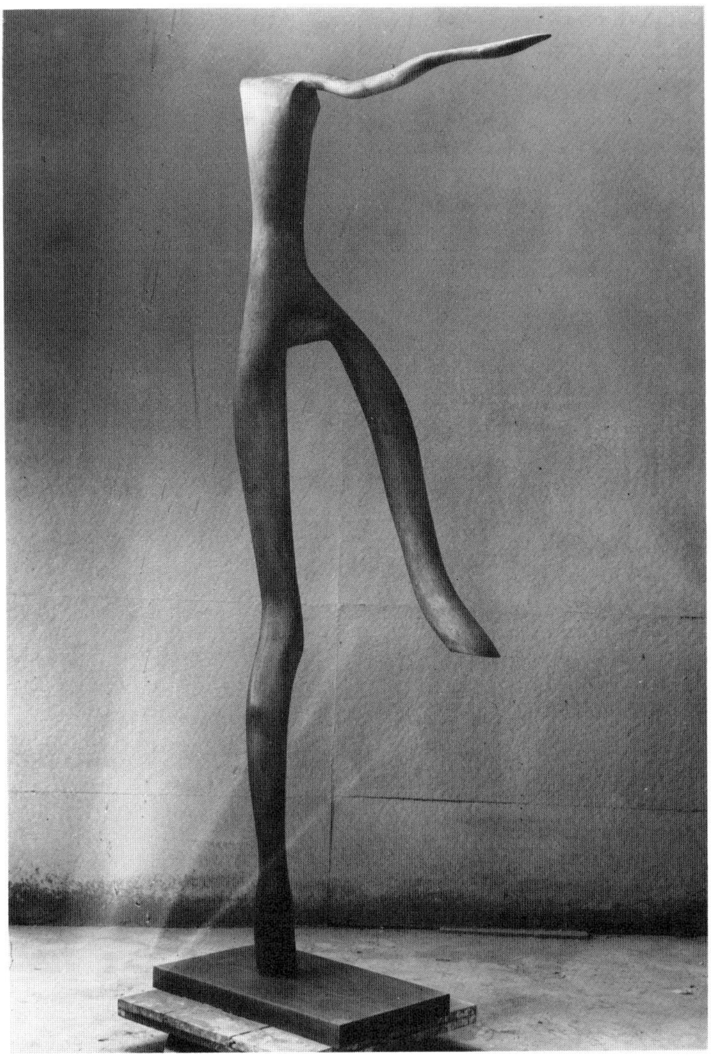

72 Daphne into Laurel
completed 1982
Plane h.86 (219)
The Artist

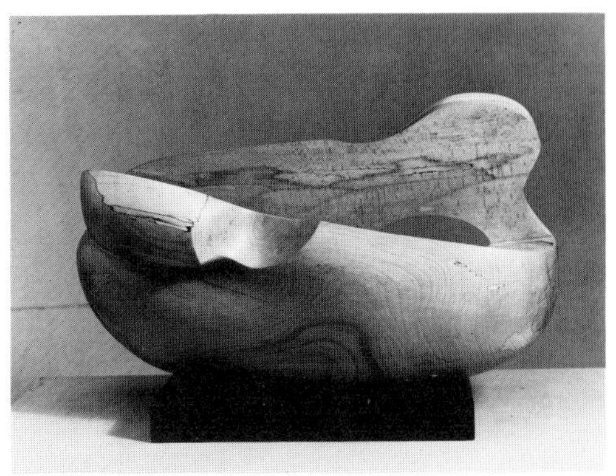

73 Saw Cut 1983
Beech l.25 ½ (64)
The Artist

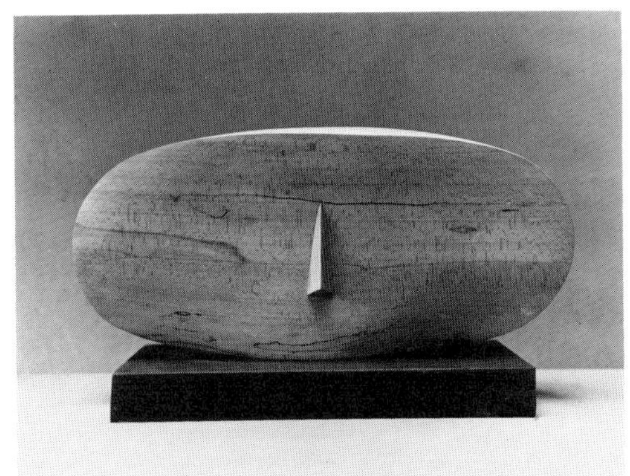

74 Horizontal Head 1983
Beech h.23 ½ (59)
Rhoda Pritzker

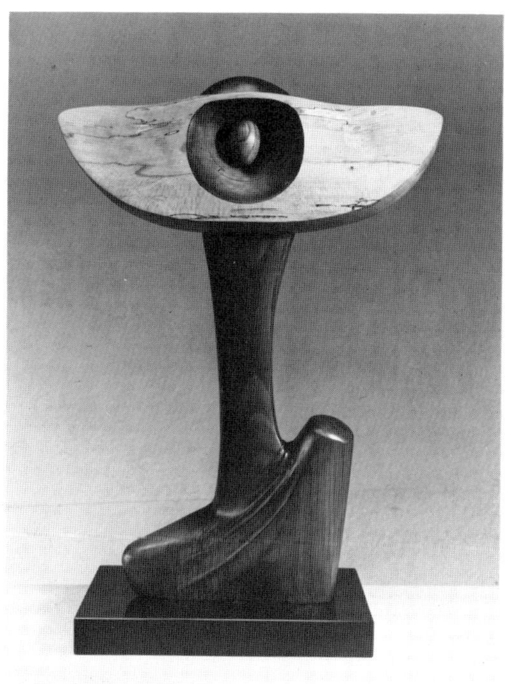

75 **Egg Head** 1983
Beech and cherry h.27 (68.5)
The Artist

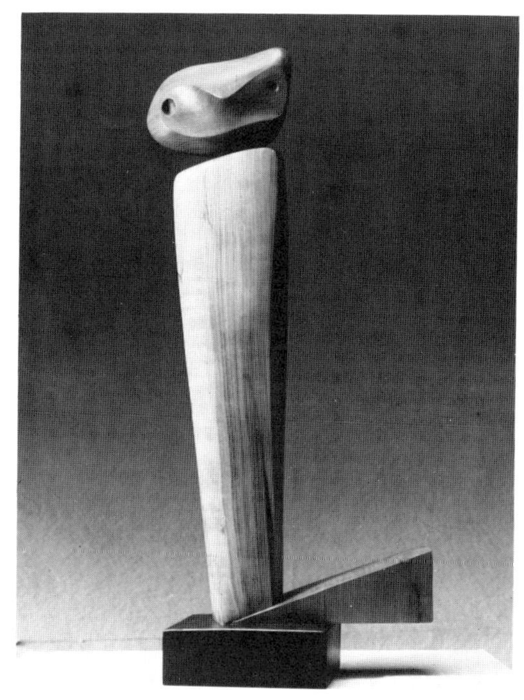

76 **The Wedge** 1983
Elm, cherry and mahogany
h.33 (84)
The Artist

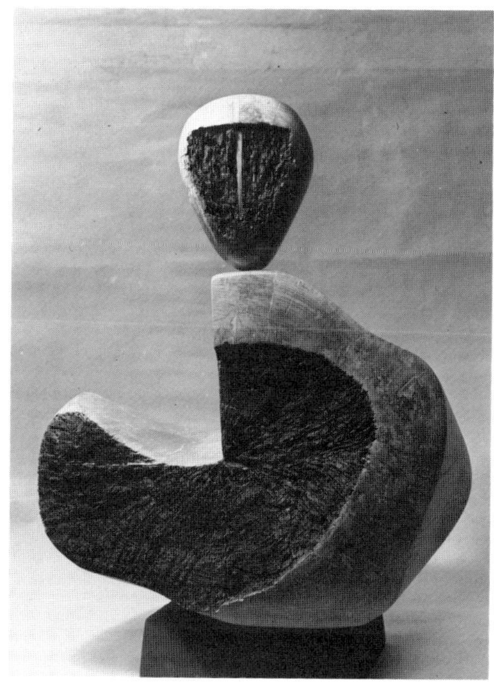

77 **Poseidon** 1986
Cherry h.26 (66)
The Artist

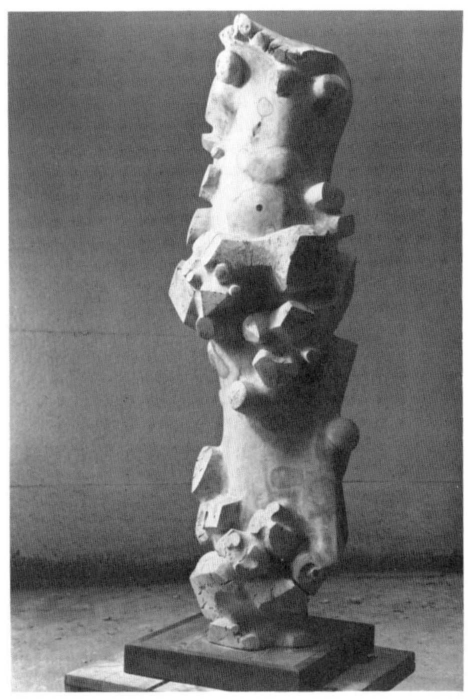

78 Mulberry Figure One 1988
Mulberry h.54 (137)
The Artist

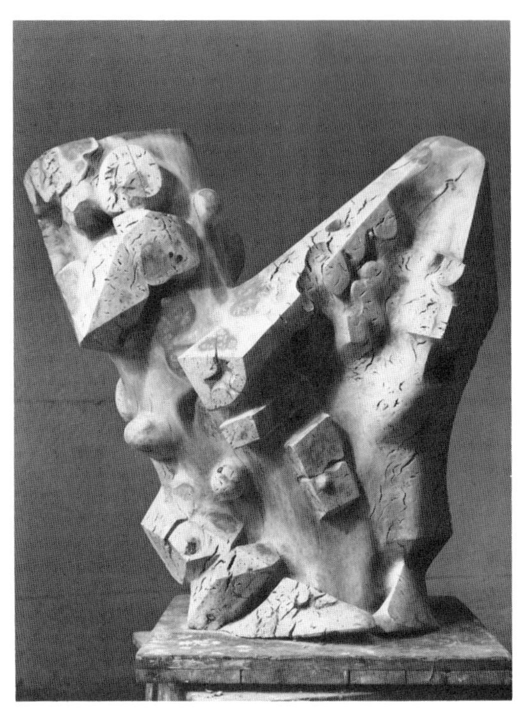

79 Mulberry Figure Two 1988
Mulberry l.35 (89)
The Artist

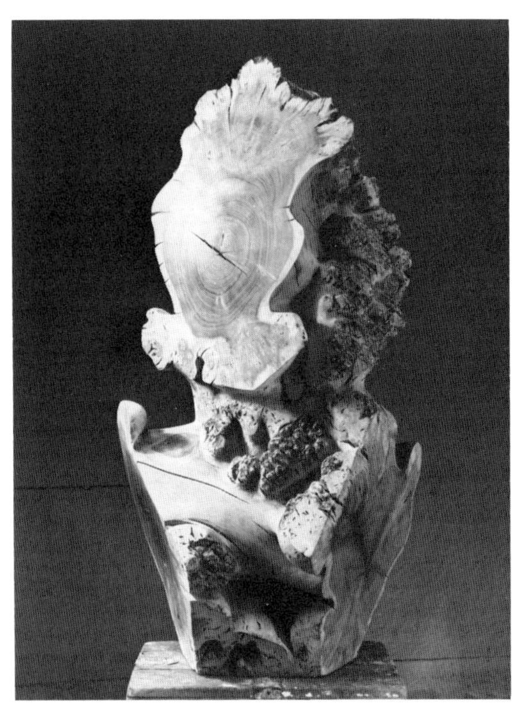

80 Mulberry Figure Three 1988
Mulberry h.41 (104)
The Artist

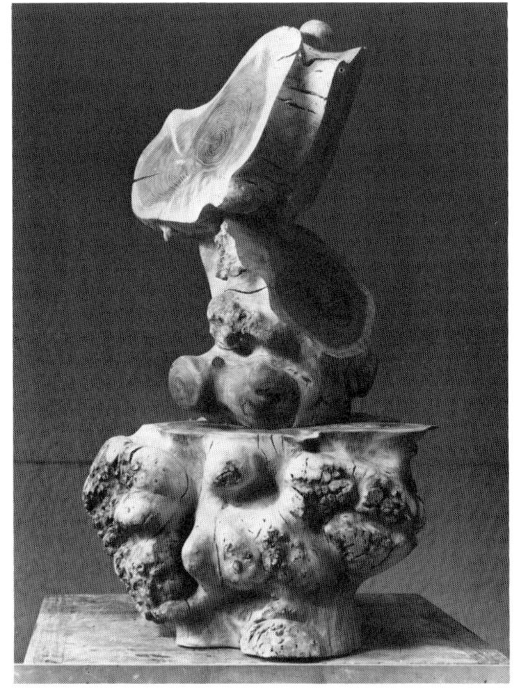

81 Mulberry Figure Four 1988
Mulberry h.31½ (80)
The Artist

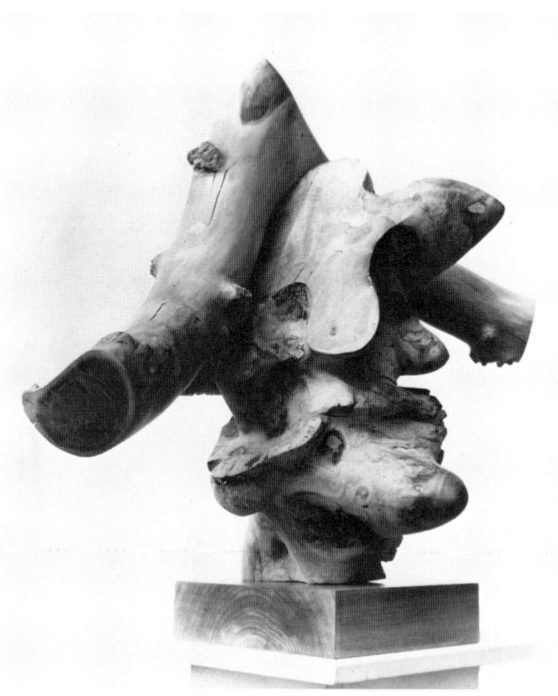

82 Mulberry Figure Five 1988
Mulberry h.24 (61)
The Artist

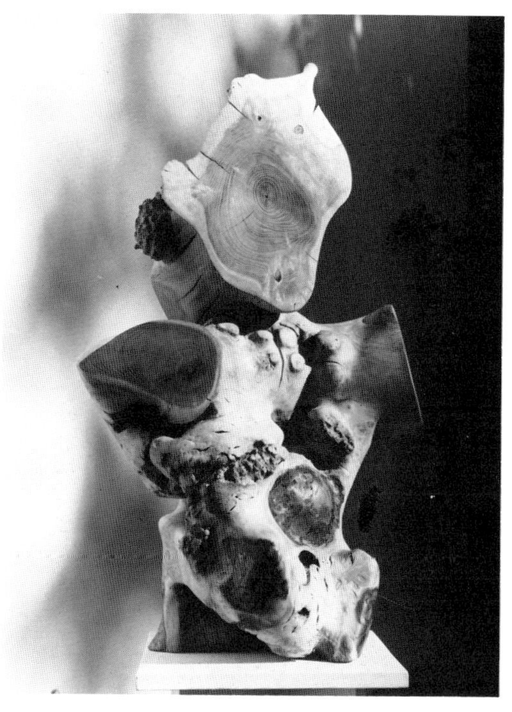

83 Mulberry Figure Six 1988
Mulberry h.29 (74)
The Artist

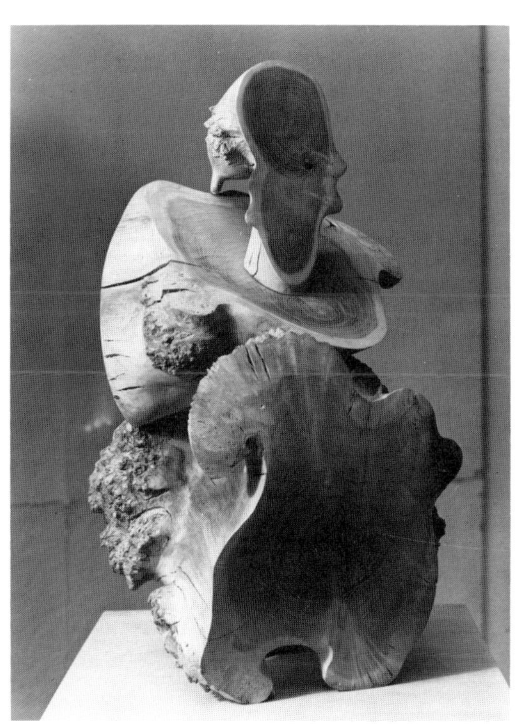

84 Mulberry Figure Seven 1988
Mulberry h.24 (61)
The Artist

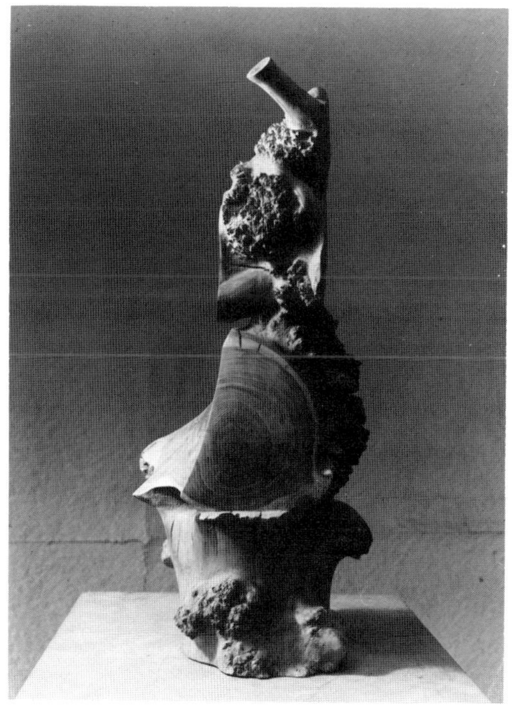

85 Mulberry Figure Eight 1988
Mulberry h.32 (81)
The Artist